So You're in Love, Now What?

20 Q&A to Help You Make the Marriage Decision

MARK D. OGLETREE, PH.D.

CFI
AN IMPRINT OF CEDAR FORT, INC.
SPRINGVILLE, UTAH

© 2022 Mark D. Ogletree
All rights reserved.

No part of this book may be reproduced in any form whatsoever, whether by graphic, visual, electronic, film, microfilm, tape recording, or any other means, without prior written permission of the publisher, except in the case of brief passages embodied in critical reviews and articles.

This is not an official publication of The Church of Jesus Christ of Latter-day Saints. The opinions and views expressed herein belong solely to the author and do not necessarily represent the opinions or views of Cedar Fort, Inc. Permission for the use of sources, graphics, and photos is also solely the responsibility of the author.

ISBN 13: 978-1-4621-4330-6

Published by CFI, an imprint of Cedar Fort, Inc.
2373 W. 700 S., Springville, UT 84663
Distributed by Cedar Fort, Inc., www.cedarfort.com

Library of Congress Control Number: 2022938945

Cover design by Courtney Proby
Cover design © 2022 Cedar Fort, Inc.
Substantive by Rachel Hathcock

Printed in the United States of America

10 9 8 7 6 5 4 3 2 1

Printed on acid-free paper

To my loving wife, Janie, who has taught me so much about marriage and family life. And to our eight children and their spouses: Brittany, Tyler, Brandon, Amanda, Bethany, Will, Maddie, James, Kenzie, Jared, Cassidy, Austin, Callie, Tanner, and Natalie. I hope that you will teach your children—our grandchildren—these same principles so that one day, they will marry as well as each of you have.

Contents

Introduction: Why Do Young People Fear Marriage?	1
What are some of the major decisions you must make?	7
How can you tell if you are in love?	13
How can you overcome the fear to marry?	21
What are some ways the Holy Ghost can speak to us?	27
What is the relationship between making our own choices and being directed by the Spirit?	35
How does the Holy Ghost work through our thoughts?	41
How does the Holy Ghost work through our feelings?	47
How can peace be a manifestation of the Spirit?	55
Are you being prompted by the Holy Ghost or your own emotions?	61
Is it true that revelation often comes in small pieces instead of large doses?	67
Can "instinct" be part of the revelatory process?	73
What is the principle of stewardship in revelation?	81
What are some barriers to feeling the Holy Ghost?	89
What is a stupor of thought?	97
How can timing affect the marriage decision?	105
How can I receive personal revelation?	111

CONTENTS

Could Heavenly Father give us confusing answers?	119
What roles can doubt, worry, and fear play in the marriage decision?	125
What if two people receive different answers?	133
Have you ever recorded a personal revelation?	143
Conclusion: Are you ready to move forward with faith?	151
About the Author	153

Introduction: Why Do Young People Fear Marriage?

Making the marriage decision can be one of the most joyous and thrilling experiences in life. However, there can also be large doses of fear and trepidation that accompany this most vital choice. Why do so many young adults fear marriage? After all, isn't marriage supposed to be fun, happy, and exciting? For the past decades, transitioning from a young single adult to marriage was a natural part of the growing up and maturing process. In years past, if you wanted to be an adult, you moved out of your parents' home, "got hitched," and rode off into the matrimonial sunset.

Today, many young singles do not feel that marriage is necessary for the transition into adulthood. Presently, only half of adults in the United States are married, compared with 72 percent in 1960.[1] Today, the percentage of young adults between the ages of 18 and 29 who are married fell from 59 percent in 1960 to 20 percent by 2010.[2] The average age of people who marry in

---

1. Kim Parker and Renee Stepler, "As U.S. Marriage Rate Hovers at 50%, Education Gap in Marital Status Widens," Pew Research Center, 14 September 2017; https://www.pewresearch.org/fact-tank/2017/09/14/as-u-s-marriage-rate-hovers-at-50-education-gap-in-marital-status-widens/
2. See D'Vera Cohn, et. al, "Barely Half of U.S. Adults Are Married—a Record Low," Pew Research Center, Social and Demographic Trends, Dec. 14, 2011, available at www.pewsocialtrends.org/2011/12/14/barely-half-of-u-s-adults-are-married-a-record-low; "Rash Retreat from Marriage," *Christian Science Monitor*, Jan. 2 and 9, 2012, 34; as cited by Elder Dallin H. Oaks, "No Other Gods," *Ensign*, November 2013, 72-75.

the United States is twenty-seven for women and twenty-nine for men.[3] A decade or two earlier, couples were marrying in their early twenties. Even in the Church, many members are waiting longer to marry. For example, at Brigham Young University, 36 percent of seniors were married in the fall semester of 2015, compared to 42 percent in the fall of 1996. Although LDS Church schools lead the way in our nation when it comes to married students in college, even Latter-day Saints are waiting longer to tie the knot.

Fear of Marriage

In one study several years ago, one-third of LDS young adults between the ages of twenty-one and twenty-five reported having some major concerns or reservations about marriage.[4] Perhaps many believe that they are not ready to take on the lofty responsibilities that accompany marriage. Others may feel that they want to continue enjoying the single life. In a study conducted by Brigham Young University researchers several years ago, students were asked to identify the "strong" factors that would cause them to delay making the marriage decision. Almost 60 percent of the students stated that the "fear of making a mistake" was their chief concern. Perhaps some young single adults have seen broken relationships and terrible marriages up close, and they simply do not want to become a divorce statistic. Maybe others do not trust their ability to determine if a relationship is "right" or approved in the eyes of God. In some cases, individuals may wonder if they are up for the lofty responsibilities that marriage brings.

---

3. Sarah Averett, "BYU Marriage Statistics Reflect US Trends, Attitudes," The Daily Universe, 1 September 2016; https://universe.byu.edu/2016/09/01/byu-marriage-statistics-reflect-us-trends-attitudes/
4. Jason S. Carroll, *Project Ready*, Brigham Young University, 2009.

INTRODUCTION

Former General Relief Society President Julie B. Beck explained:

> We know, from our studies here at Church headquarters concerning the rising generation, that our youth are increasingly less confident in the institution of families. They are less confident in their ability to form a successful eternal family. Because they are less confident in families, they're placing more and more value on education and less and less importance on forming an eternal family.[5]

Getting married and forming families takes faith. In fact, in one sense, to get married is to step into the darkness and look for the light. Sometimes, couples may lack the assurance that marriage will work for them, or if they will be able to afford marriage. For example, Janie and I were married during the month of April many years ago. I remembered going into that week of our wedding wondering how everything was going to work out. I was most concerned about money. We both had no more than some loose change in our wallets. The thought of asking our parents for financial help never occurred to either of us. I was waiting for a four-hundred-dollar tax return to provide some funds for us to travel to the Houston area for our wedding reception. Thankfully, that money came the day before our wedding. I am happy to report that everything worked out, and we made it safely to Houston. Some gift money given at our reception in Texas allowed us to travel back to Provo. If not for those wonderful wedding gifts of cash, we may still be living in the Lone Star State. However, things have a way of working out. The Lord watches over us, especially when we strive do His will.

Getting married is certainly an exercise of faith, belief, and hope. Of course, there are many other concerns besides money,

---

5. Julie B. Beck, *Teaching the Doctrine of the Family,* Seminaries and Institutes of Religion Satellite Broadcast, 4 August 2009, 3–4.

including how you will get along with each other, how you will deal with your parents, when you will begin your family, whether you made the right decision, and one hundred other worries. I recommend that you do not focus on everything that could possibly go wrong but concentrate on the many things that are right, good, and wonderful about the relationship.

Dr. Bruce A. Chadwick, a former professor of sociology at Brigham Young University, declared in a devotional address, that we must do the following:

> *Exercise faith and to have courage in dating and marriage.* It is scary to marry! It is scary to stay married during troubled times! It is scary to be responsible for children! Some people are afraid of marriage and parenthood. Perhaps their parents or close friends divorced and they fear the same is happening to them.
>
> Have faith in God your Father and in His Son. They will guide and strengthen us because we are on their errand of creating eternal families and raising children in righteousness. This message is simply stated in the words of President Ezra Taft Benson to young adults: "Those fears must be replaced with faith" ("To the Single Adult Brethren of the Church," *Ensign*, May 1988, 52).[6]

Indeed, it can be scary to marry and to raise a family in our contemporary world. There are so many issues that couples must navigate to raise a successful family in a toxic environment. Nevertheless, the Lord will take care of you. He wants you to marry. He wants you to form families, and He will bless you. Just watch—things will work out. Replace your fears with faith. Over the years, I have observed many couples who have made the decision to marry. In many cases, impossible situations have been

---

6. Dr. Bruce A. Chadwick, "Hanging Out, Hooking Up, and Celestial Marriage," *Brigham Young University Speeches*, 7 May 2002; https://speeches.byu.edu/talks/bruce-a-chadwick/hanging-hooking-celestial-marriage/

resolved, difficult challenges have been overcome, and things seem to work themselves out. Prior to the wedding day, individuals are able to sell their apartment contracts, miraculously find married housing, and figure out a way to pay for their expenses. In addition, some of the gifts they receive at the reception are just what the doctor ordered. Almost magically, their new apartment is furnished, their cupboards are full, and they have enough gas in their car to get them around town for another week.

How will you discover if marrying the person you are in love with is right for you and approved by God? Do you feel comfortable receiving answers from the Spirit? In the same study I referred to earlier, Brigham Young University students were asked how they planned to make the marriage decision. Some responded that they would "know" they had found the right person because it "feels right" or "we enjoy spending time together." Others mentioned a "feeling of love" or "compatibility." Nevertheless, the number-one answer was "spiritual confirmation." However, I was surprised that only 22 percent of the men and 29 percent of the women said that is how they would know they were marrying the right person. In fact, I expected that almost all would come to know if their marriage decision was correct by a manifestation of the Spirit. I was just as surprised that the third most common response to "how will you make the marriage decision" was "other." I am not sure what "other" means—if that is "rock, paper, scissors," a Magic 8 Ball, or a message in a fortune cookie.

As I have visited with my students at Brigham Young University over the past ten years, I have discovered that although most of them have served missions, many do not feel comfortable receiving answers from the Spirit. Some may lack experience in being led by the Spirit, while others do not trust the spiritual process. Others are unfamiliar with how the Spirit works in their lives. In fact, some have even claimed that they have never felt the guidance of the Holy Ghost—ever. No wonder former Relief Society President Sister Julie B. Beck stated that to learn to hear the voice of the Holy Ghost, and then act on it, is "the single most important skill that can be acquired in this life."[7]

I believe that most of my students have actually felt the Spirit and have had spiritual experiences in their lives—they just did not know that they were feeling the Spirit. Many of them have never been taught how the Holy Ghost manifests Himself to them. Others have not made major decisions in their lives without their parents leading and directing the way. For whatever reason, many young single adults have never been taught how to make major decisions or how to receive answers to their prayers. Learning to understand the promptings of the Spirit and then to follow the inspiration we receive takes time and effort.

The purpose of this book is to help you navigate your way through the marriage decision. I want to provide you with tools, insights, doctrines, and experiences that can help you with this process. Years ago, President Spencer W. Kimball taught that when making the marriage decision, the most careful planning, thinking, praying, and fasting should be employed. He then stated of all the decisions in life, "this one must not be wrong."[8] The primary purpose of this book is to help you make the marriage decision with confidence and certainty. The key to that kind of spiritual confidence is learning to receive answers from the Holy Ghost.

Thought Questions

1. What are some of the major decisions you have had to make in your life?
2. How did you come to know those decisions were correct?

---

7. Julie B. Beck, *Ensign*, May 2010, 11.
8. President Spencer W. Kimball, "Oneness in Marriage," *Ensign*, March 1977, 3.

1

What are some of the major decisions you must make?

It is remarkable, and somewhat overwhelming, to consider all of the major decisions in life that could be made before a faithful Latter-day Saint reaches the age of twenty-five. The first major decisions seem to come between the ages of seventeen and eighteen. Some of those decisions include:

- Will I attend college?
- Where will I attend college?
- Will I serve a mission?
- When should I submit my mission papers?

After one returns home from their mission, other major decisions include:

- What should I major in?
- Whom should I date?
- Whom should I marry? When will we marry? In which temple should our marriage take place?
- Where will we live once we are married?
- Should we both work and attend school once we are married?

- When should we begin to start our family?
- Where should I work? Should we both work?

As individuals conclude their undergraduate schooling, other decisions to consider include:

- Should I (we) attend graduate school?
- How will we pay for graduate school? Should we take out student loans?
- What should I study in graduate school?
- Where will we live while in graduate school?

Then of course, after graduate school, there are other monumental decisions, such as:

- What job offer should we accept? What if we do not have a job offer?
- How many more children should we have?
- How will we pay off our student loans?
- Should we buy a home?
- Where would we like to settle down and live more permanently?

It is amazing that most of these monumental decisions occur within such a short time span. President Thomas S. Monson stated, "I cannot stress too strongly that decisions determine destiny. You can't make eternal decisions without eternal consequences."[1] The decisions that we make can drastically affect both the course and the outcome of our lives. Small decisions can transition into significant consequences.

---

1. Thomas S. Monson, "Decisions Determine Destiny," *Brigham Young University Speeches*, 6 November 2005; https://speeches.byu.edu/talks/thomas-s-monson/decisions-determine-destiny/

WHAT ARE SOME OF THE MAJOR DECISIONS YOU MUST MAKE?

In our families, and in certain Church settings, perhaps we could do more to prepare young single adults to successfully navigate their way through these life-changing decisions. I remember the hours of thought, deliberation, exploration, and prayer that went into deciding upon my career. I spent many hours talking to professionals and friends about potential jobs. Of course, there were other serious decisions that we struggled to resolve. I remember spending many hours with Janie, trying to decide what course of action we would follow pertaining career, graduate school, children, and where to live. Perhaps the most significant aspect of this process were spiritual interventions we employed, such as fasting, prayer, and attending the temple.

I remember one day praying on the backside of the Hill Cumorah for answers regarding my career path. Before you think that I made a pilgrimage to Palmyra to receive such an answer, I should clarify that along with Janie and her family, we were there as participants in the Hill Cumorah Pageant. I had some extra time one afternoon, so I hiked around the back of the hill, away from the noise of all who were there, and poured my heart out in prayer. I returned to Janie with great confidence in what I should do professionally. I have never regretted that decision to work in the field of religious education. It was amazing how once that decision was made, everything seemed to fall into place.

A couple of months after that prayer, I was offered a job to work as a full-time seminary teacher in Mesa, Arizona. Our next big decision centered on where we would live. We did not have many choices in those days. It would have been "Apartment #1" or "Apartment #2." I vividly remember sitting with Janie in a Dairy Queen in Mesa and making a pros and cons list for each apartment. After weighing out the options over dip cones, we chose Apartment #1, and that seemed to make all the difference. Even though we moved out of that apartment three months later into our first house, living in that apartment helped us to understand the geographic area where we wanted to live. About a year after that experience, we faced our next major decisions with graduate school. Later, we had to decide on the number of children we should have, if my career path would suit us in the long term, and where we would live permanently and ultimately raise our family. Undoubtedly, it sometimes seems that life consists of one major decision after the other.[2]

Of course, there are bigger decisions in life other than where to live or what job opportunities to accept. I believe the marriage decision is perhaps the most crucial decision of all. Whom you marry affects everything you will ultimately do. It will influence your happiness. It will affect how you serve in the Church and build the kingdom. It will affect how your children turn out. It could even affect your career. Years ago, President Spencer W. Kimball declared, "Marriage is perhaps the most vital of all decisions and has the most far-reaching effects, for it has to do not only with immediate happiness, but also with eternal joys. It affects not only the two people involved, but also their families and particularly their children and their children's children down through many generations."[3]

Recently I met with one of my students who wanted to ask me a question. He said, "Dr. Ogletree, my dad said that I have permission to ask you this question for him. He is not sure what to do because my mother will *not* let him serve in the Church. He is active and faithful, and at this stage in his life, many of his friends serve in the Young Men's Program, some serve in bishoprics, and others in elders quorum presidencies. But my mom will not let my dad serve in the Church, and he's really sad about it."

I felt sad for the father who wanted desperately to serve in the Church and help build the kingdom. After all, he had made covenants that he would put the Lord first in his life and serve

---

2. See Mark D. Ogletree, *Preparing for Your Celestial Marriage* (American Fork, UT: Covenant Communications, 2017), 6–7.
3. Spencer W. Kimball, "Oneness in Marriage," *Ensign*, March 1977, 3.

Him faithfully. I explained to my student that this situation was certainly a difficult one, and I recommended to him that his parents should at least visit with their bishop about the matter, or perhaps even consider marriage counseling. Serving in the Church can bring love, life, unity, and energy to a marriage.

Because the marriage decision is so crucial, every Latter-day Saint should consult with the Lord and receive His guidance. The Holy Ghost can give you assurance and provide peace in the midst of difficult decisions. Many years ago, Elder Marion G. Romney of the Quorum of the Twelve Apostles taught a principle that I completely believe:

> Now, I tell you that you can make every decision in your life correctly if you can learn to follow the guidance of the Holy Spirit. . . . Study your problems and prayerfully make a decision. Then take that decision and say to him, in a simple, honest supplication, "Father, I want to make the right decision. I want to do the right thing. This is what I think I should do: let me know if it is the right course." Doing this, you can get the burning in your bosom, if your decision is right. If you do not get the burning, then change your decision and submit a new one. When you learn to walk by the Spirit, you never need to make a mistake.[4]

A significant key to receiving revelation is worthiness. If an individual keeps the commandments and repents daily, they can enjoy the constant influence of the Holy Ghost. If that individual seeks the Spirit, they will receive the guidance the Lord has promised. With the Lord's guidance, we never need to make a mistake. The Lord loves us, and He wants to reveal His will to us. He wants to direct our lives and help us with such large decisions that affect eternity. Stay close to the Lord, and He will stay close to you. He will direct you into places and

---

4. Elder Marion G. Romney, *Conference Report*, October 1961, 60–61.

situations where you and your loved ones can thrive. Because the marriage decision is so crucial, I have no doubt that He will help you get it right.

Thought Questions

1. What is the biggest decision you have had to make in your life? How did you go about deciding what to do?
2. What guidance have you felt from the Lord in your decision-making?

2

How can you tell if you are in love?

Some of you may remember the experience Elder Boyd K. Packer shared about a conversation he had with an atheist. The two men were sitting next to each other on an airplane, and the atheist insisted that Elder Packer could *not know* that there was a God. After some deep conversation, Elder Packer asked the atheist if he could explain what salt tastes like. As you may remember, the atheist was baffled that he could not explain the taste of salt.[1]

Over the years, I have decided that explaining what love is can be just as difficult. Do you know what it means to be in love? Could you describe it? I have been in the business of marriage and family for more than thirty years, and I am not sure if I could explain to you what it means to be in love. It may be easier to identify the elements that constitute love, which we will do in this chapter.

Several years ago, researchers wanted to understand how individuals perceive "being in love." A questionnaire was administered to college students, and the results were intriguing. The students could not agree on how to describe love. In fact, some students admitted that they did not know what love was. One student in the survey said, "Love is like lightning—you may not

---

1. See Elder Boyd K. Packer, "The Candle of the Lord," *Ensign,* January 1983.

know what it is, but you know it when it hits you."[2] And perhaps that is the best answer—when you are in love, you will know it!

Elements of Love

Elder Richard G. Scott taught that love elevates, protects, respects, and enriches another. He added that love also "motivates one to make sacrifices for another."[3] Love is certainly less about us and more about giving of ourselves. The descriptors that Elder Scott mentions are certainly some of the elements of love, although the list is probably not all-inclusive. Selflessness appears to be a significant component of love, as well as sacrifice. Other elements of love could include compassion, service, forgiveness, charity, admiration, intimacy, and commitment. In describing charity, which is akin to love, the Apostle Paul explained that those who love "suffer long," "are kind," "envy not," are "not puffed up," "[do] not behave inappropriately," "[seek] not her own," "[are] not easily provoked," and "[think] no evil" (1 Corinthians 13:4–6). These descriptors would also be elements of true love.

LDS Perspectives on True Love

As Latter-day Saints, we have some unique perspectives on romantic love. For example, our theology teaches us that true love continues to grow with time. Hence, true love is always gaining momentum. It is building, not diminishing. This does not mean that couples cannot have bad days. In fact, occasionally some couples may not even like each other that much on a particular day. However, the trajectory of true love is most often moving upward. That is, true love is increasing and gaining steam.

---

2. Les & Leslie Parrott, *Saving Your Marriage Before it Starts* (Zondervan: Grand Rapids, Michigan, 2015), 41.
3. Scott, 1991.

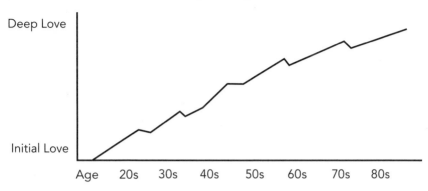

This is why couples who have been married for a while can look back on their relationship and recognize that they love each other more today than they did twenty years ago. I have been married to Janie for more than thirty-seven years. When I look back on our early days together, I wonder if we even knew each other that well. Now, after years of diapers, toddlers, teenagers, laughter, tears, sickness, health, money, and a host of other significant events, the love we feel for each other is very deep. In fact, if you are in love with someone right now, ask yourself, "Do I love them now more than I did last month, or the month before?" Why is this concept important? Because it is a doctrinal truth. True love is deep and abiding, and it is constantly gaining momentum.

President George Q. Cannon explained,

> We believe that when a man and woman are united as husband and wife, and they love each other, their hearts and feelings are one, that that love is as enduring as eternity itself, and that when death overtakes them it will neither extinguish nor cool that love, but that it will brighten and kindle it to a purer flame, and that it will endure through eternity.[4]

---

4. George Q. Cannon, *Journal of Discourses*, 14:320.

Therefore, when I meet Janie on the other side of the veil, our love will not have diminished or even remained constant—it will actually have grown. After death, when we are reunited, we will discover that we love each other more than we could have had imagined. I think that is one of the greatest concepts of romantic love ever taught. For those who are dating seriously or contemplating marriage, look for this pattern. True love increases with time.

Our theology also teaches us that righteous living increases our capacity to love. Elder Orson Pratt declared, "The more righteous a people become the more they are qualified for loving others and rendering them happy."[5] Righteous living taps us into the Savior's love, power, and strength. Keeping our covenants and observing the commandments equips us to radiate the love of Jesus Christ to our spouses and children. His love can be powerful, overwhelming, unconditional, and indestructible. The closer we draw to the Savior, the greater our capacity to love another person.

Indicators of Love

As you may have noticed, I still have not defined love. I have only provided synonyms, such as *sacrifice, selflessness,* and *compassion*. Dictionary definitions include words such as *affection, attraction, sexual desire, admiration,* and *attachment*. Perhaps instead of trying to define love, I could simply describe some components of true love. Look for these indicators as you begin to feel that you are falling in love with your significant other:

1. **Chemistry:** Chemistry explains the connection that you enjoy together. You can talk with relative ease. Laughter comes naturally, and you feel so comfortable with each other that you can simply be yourself.

---

5. Orson Pratt, "Celestial Marriage," *The Seer*, October 1853, 156.

2. ***Attraction:*** Attraction is certainly physical. You appreciate and admire each other's physical attributes. However, you can also find yourself attracted to another individual's personality, drive, ambition, sense of humor, and spiritual potential. Look for another person's entire package when it comes to attraction—not merely physical traits.
3. ***Affection:*** When affection is appropriate, you will feel especially drawn toward each other romantically. You will enjoy physical affection within the proper bounds. You may find that it is difficult *not* to touch, hold, or kiss each other.
4. ***Friendship:*** You can know that you are in love when you find yourselves becoming best friends. You discover that there is no one else that you would rather spend time with, talk to, and share in activities together. In some ways, it may feel you have known each other much longer than you really have.
5. ***Happiness:*** Does the relationship bring you happiness and joy? Do you look toward the future with each other with joy and optimism? Do you love being together?
6. ***Faith:*** Your relationship is marked by faith, not fear. You have great faith in each other, but you also have the faith that you are supposed to be together and that Heavenly Father approves of your relationship. You do not spend excessive amounts of time worrying if being together is the right thing.
7. ***Acceptance:*** You are not trying to change your partner; you are not trying to make them into something they are not. You accept them for who they are, and you love them, despite their weaknesses and challenges.
8. ***Future:*** Your goals and dreams align. You discover that you want many of the same things in life. You can see yourselves building a wonderful life together. You look forward to being together for eternity.

9. ***Improvement:*** You find that you each inspire each other. You want to improve and be better because of your partner. You find that your desire to accomplish more and to be successful is deeply connected to your significant other.
10. ***Sacrifice:*** You understand that true love is built on sacrifice. You find that you do not mind making sacrifices for your partner because you want to be together. You may find yourself giving up certain things in your life so that you can spend time with the one you love.

Recently, I sat in my counseling office with a young man who was graduating from Brigham Young University. Part of his quandary was that he was about to accept his first job offer in the Midwestern United States and would be moving shortly after graduation. At the same time, he was dating a girl rather seriously and knew that she still had several years left until she would be able to graduate. I asked him questions such as, "Is your girlfriend going to move to Iowa with you?" and "Will you come back to Utah to see her often?" To these questions and several others, he said, "You know, I think I'm going to break up with her. It would take too much work to keep our relationship moving forward, and I won't have the time to devote to that with my new job."

I then said to the young man, "Guess what, you're not in love, and that's probably a good thing. If you were in love, you would do everything in your power to keep the relationship alive—even if you lived in different states. You would be willing to make every sacrifice necessary to preserve the relationship. The fact that you do not really seem to care is an indicator to me that you are not in love."

The young man simply responded, "Yeah, you're probably right," and that was the end of our conversation, which was another indicator of his lack of investment or interest in her. Yes, sacrifice is a key indicator of true love.

Many years ago, Elder John A. Widtsoe said that the final test of true love is sacrifice.[6] You fall in love with someone when you make sacrifices for them. I learned this lesson as a new father. The day after our first baby was born, a neighbor came over to our home to see my wife and our new child. I explained that they were still at the hospital but would be coming home the next day. The neighbor then said, "How does it feel to be a father?"

I lied and said, "It feels great!"

In reality, I did not feel much about my new role. How could I have? I had not done anything yet. Yes, I was excited, but I did not feel much different than I did the days before Janie delivered our baby. However, that all changed quickly once Janie and our baby came home. As I began to make sacrifices, I started to feel like a real dad. I would hold our baby often and rock her to sleep. I would change her diapers. I would stay up late at night with her so Janie could get some sleep. Before long, I realized that the love I felt for my little girl was growing daily. The more sacrifices I made for my wife and daughter, the deeper my love grew. Indeed, true love is built on the principle of sacrifice. The more we sacrifice, the more we love.

Thought Questions

1. How will you know that you are really in love with someone?
2. What do you feel is one of the most important aspects of loving a marriage partner? How will you show your love to them?

---

6. John A. Widtsoe, "An Understandable Religion," 72.

3

How can you overcome the fear to marry?

In our present world, we are surrounded by fear from every direction, and perhaps many of those fears are justified. After all, we have recently experienced a global pandemic, political instability, natural disasters, wars, and a host of other calamities. The tendency to fear also trickles into our personal lives on many different levels. For instance, many individuals let fear paralyze them from making decisions that could ultimately make them happy—especially the marriage decision.

Several years ago, researchers at Brigham Young University asked students, "What are some 'strong' causes for you to delay marriage?" Almost 800 students responded to this question in the survey. According to this data, the number-one cause for BYU students to delay marriage was the fear of making a mistake (59 percent of men; 58 percent of women).[1] I have asked my students what they fear the most regarding marriage. Although some say that they fear selecting a "wrong" marriage partner, most fear the possibility of divorce or having a poor marriage. Many of these students grew up in homes where they saw firsthand the

---

1. B.A. Chadwick, B.L. Top, and R.J. McClendon, *Shield of Faith: The Power of Religion in the Lives of LDS Youth and Young Adults* (Salt Lake City: Deseret Book, 2010), 244.

consequences of divorce, or at least the challenges of sub-par marriages. Unfortunately, many have bought into the mistaken belief that because their parents had a difficult marriage, by default they are destined to follow their parents' footsteps. Many do not realize that this belief does not have to be true.

Not long ago, I met with a student in my office. On the surface, he seemed like a powerful and polished returned missionary, ready to take on the world and anything that stood in his way. Underneath all of that, however, was a young man who lived in fear. He was afraid of the future, marriage, and the prospects of family. He sobbed as he told me about his broken and dysfunctional family. He told me stories about abuse, infidelity, drugs, alcohol, illegitimate births, divorce, and of ultimately being raised by a single mother in a small home "on the other side of the tracks." He looked at me and through his tears told me he had no idea how to be a good father and a good husband. He did not have any faith that he could overcome his past life.

I assured this young man that he had every right to believe that he could be wonderful in both of those critical roles—husband and father. First, I assured him that growing up in those circumstances did not mean he would repeat history—not at all. In fact, I promised him that he would be a "cycle breaker" and change the trajectory of his family history. This revelation is for everyone: *Just because you grew up in a broken home, saw divorce firsthand, or were raised in a household with a rotten marriage, that does not have to mean that you will repeat that pattern.*

I was raised in a home with parents who had a difficult marriage. My mother and father fought and argued on a regular basis. Since I was the oldest sibling, my mother would often pay me to take my siblings to a movie or do something fun. She wanted to be able to argue with my dad without children in the way. When they finally divorced, I was grateful that I would not have to hear them fight, yell, and scream one more day. As a teenager, I recognized that I wanted more for my future marriage. I wanted a wife that I adored and cherished, and would be my best friend. I visualized being married and showing love and affection to each other, as well as laughing together each day. I would tell myself that when I married, I would just do exactly the opposite of what my parents did, and I would probably have a great relationship with my spouse.

That formula has proven to be effective. Although Janie and I do not have a perfect marriage—no one does—we have a very happy marriage and family life. In fact, our life is the exact opposite of the home life I experienced as a child and adolescent. For those who grew up in a similar situation to me, I promise there is great hope for you and your future spouse to form a healthy and successful marriage and family life. Do not ever be chained, fettered, and held hostage by the past. We are here on this earth life to act and not be acted upon! (see 2 Nephi 2:26). Therefore, we do not need to be victims of our past. We can become the architects of a great future, filled with hope and faith.

Now back to the interview with my student. I told my student that if he placed Jesus Christ at the center of his life and the center of his family, he would be on the road to having a wonderful family life. Having a Christ-centered home alleviates, and can even prevent, a multitude of problems. Finally, I told him that because he deeply desired to be a good husband and father, I believed he would be. I believe desire is 90 percent of the battle. If we deeply desire something, if it is a righteous desire, the Lord will help us obtain that desire (see Mormon 9:18–21). I explained to my student that if he intentionally worked hard to be a good father and husband, read books about family life and marriage, found good mentors who had solid marriage and families, and then practiced what he learned, he would one day be an outstanding family man. Elder Earl C. Tingey promised, "For some, [marriage and family] would appear impossible to obtain. But please have faith, and join that faith with works. The Lord is aware of you as individuals and of your particular circumstances. He will bless you. He will assist you in bringing to pass that which is right and which you righteously desire."[2] The Lord will honor our righteous desires, especially if we chose each day to honor him.

Speaking of desire, Elder John A. Widtsoe taught:

> If we want something for this Church, and Kingdom, or if we want something for our individual lives, we must have a great, earnest, overpowering desire for that thing. We must reach out for it, with full faith in our Heavenly Father that the gift may be given us. Then it would seem as if the Lord himself cannot resist our petition. If our desire is strong enough, if our whole will is tempered and attuned to that which we desire, if our lives make us worthy of the desired gift, the Lord, by his own words, is bound to give us that which we desire, in his own time and in his own manner.[3]

Our desires can mold us and shape us into the kind of individuals we want to be. If our desires are healthy, righteous, and good, I am convinced the Lord will help us obtain those desires. On the other hand, if you believe that your marriage will fail, or that you may become a divorce statistic because someone in your family is divorced, then you are living in fear, not faith. To believe that you are certain to divorce is a victim mentality.

Furthermore, Elder Jeffrey R. Holland taught us that we should believe in "good things to come."[4] Therefore, focusing on the potential destruction and remote possibility of divorce is a very unhealthy way to live. So, learn to live by faith, not by fear. Focus on the good, believe in yourself, and believe in your future spouse. Elder Jeffrey R. Holland further explained:

---

2. Earl C. Tingey, "The Simple Truths from Heaven—the Lord's Pattern," CES Fireside for Young Adults, 13 January 2008.
3. John A. Widtsoe, *Conference Report*, April 1935, 82.
4. Jeffrey R. Holland, "An High Priest of Good Things To Come," *Ensign*, November 1999.

We must never, in any age or circumstance, let fear and the father of fear (Satan himself), divert us from our faith and faithful living. There have always been questions about the future. Every young person or every young couple in every era has had to walk by faith into what has always been some uncertainty—starting with Adam and Eve in those tremulous steps out of the Garden of Eden. But that is all right. This is the plan. It will be okay. Just be faithful. God is in charge. He knows your name and He knows your need.[5]

The Lord knows us! What an incredible revelation. He loves us, because we are His children. Moreover, He wants us to be successful. God does not want us to fail. He wants us to succeed, and He will help us along the way. He will always be there for us. As we pour out our hearts to Him in prayer, He will give us strength, support, and the help we need to fulfill our goals and dreams. For that to happen, we need to believe Him, trust Him, love Him, and strive to become more like our Heavenly Father.

Thought Questions

1. What do you fear the most about marriage?
2. How do you plan to overcome your fears about marriage, and exercise faith?

---

5. Holland, "Terror, Triumph, and a Wedding Feast," *Brigham Young University Speeches*, 12 September 2004, 3.

4

What are some ways the Holy Ghost can speak to us?

What most individuals desire as they progress toward marriage is to receive a witness from the Holy Ghost that the path they are pursuing is correct, and they want the Lord to confirm or sustain their marriage decision. Unfortunately, many members of the Church, including myself, do not always understand when the Spirit is speaking to them. In some cases, we have been taught about the manifestations of the Spirit in incorrect ways. For example, some individuals in our wards and stakes talk openly about spiritual manifestations, misleading some to believe that magnificent, spiritual experiences come frequently. Moreover, they often use phrases such as:

- "The Spirit spoke to me and said . . ."
- "The Spirit told me to tell you . . ."
- "The Spirit is telling me right now that . . .
- "The Spirit told me to turn left at the intersection, instead of right . . ."

Such expressions can be intimidating to those who feel the Spirit in less dramatic ways. In fact, some individuals may feel or think that they should "turn left" instead of "right" at a certain intersection, but may have never supposed that was the Spirit directing them. Years ago, I had a missionary in my zone relate to me that the Spirit told him how to untie a knot in his shoelace. Such dramatic conceptualizations of the Holy Ghost can be confusing to those who experience spiritual manifestations in less remarkable ways, especially to those of us who simply figure out how to untie our shoes on our own. I know the Holy Ghost could tell us how to get a knot out of a shoelace, but I also believe the Lord gave us our minds to think and reason. Moreover, dramatic, spiritual experiences are not that common.

Elder Boyd K. Packer taught, "I have learned that strong, impressive spiritual experiences do not come to us very frequently. And when they do, they are generally for our own edification, instruction, or correction. Unless we are called by proper authority to do so, they do not position us to counsel or correct others."[1] For most of us, the Holy Ghost will speak to us in less dramatic ways—ways that are simple, and in some cases, even ordinary. For example, years ago, our oldest daughter came home from Church quite frustrated. We were having our Sunday family dinner, and our daughter, Brittany, said, "Well, I guess I do not have a testimony?" Janie and I asked her why she felt that way. Brittany explained that in Young Women class that day, they had a testimony meeting. Every girl was crying, and so was each leader. Our daughter was the only person in the room who did not shed a tear. From that experience, she assumed she was spiritually broken. Brittany did not understand that there are many ways the Spirit can speak to us—and most manifestations are not dramatic. That Sunday afternoon, we helped Brittany understand two things. First, just because everyone was crying did not necessarily mean that they were feeling the Spirit. As a bishop, I have attended plenty of "campfire-testimony meetings" at girls camps over the years. Most of us understand that once

---

1. Boyd K. Packer, "The Candle of the Lord," *Ensign*, January 1983.

the first girl begins to cry, it is like a "snowball" effect going through the entire group. Some girls will even say in their testimony, "I don't even know why I'm crying." In our stake last summer, one girl said, "I guess I'm crying because I'm tired, hungry, and haven't taken a shower in a week." I told her that would cause me to cry as well.

Second, we taught our daughter that tears are not always associated with feeling the Spirit—but can be for some. For example, my wife cries every time the Spirit comes upon her. Others may cry more sporadically. That day, we helped our daughter understand that there are many ways we can feel the Spirit. On that special Sabbath day, we taught her some the different manifestations of the Holy Ghost. Since then, we have tried to teach all of our children the same principles. For those of you desiring a spiritual confirmation regarding the marriage decision, these same principles apply. It will be helpful to understand the different ways the Spirit can speak to you. Perhaps more importantly, recognize that the manifestations from the Holy Ghost most often come in subtle, quiet, less dramatic ways. Pay attention to quiet, simple promptings from the Holy Ghost.[2]

The Workings of the Holy Ghost

President Martin Van Buren asked Joseph Smith what the difference was between our church and other churches. Joseph taught the president that the difference was that we had the Holy Ghost and that "all other considerations were contained in that gift."[3] That was a bold statement, but Joseph never shied away from the truth. As members of The Church of Jesus Christ of Latter-day Saints, we have that precious gift of the Spirit with

---

2. See Mark D. Ogletree, *Preparing for Your Celestial Marriage* (American Fork, Utah: Covenant Communications, 2017) 193–94.
3. Joseph Smith, *History of the Church*, 4:42.

us. Our challenge is to stay worthy so that we can enjoy the constant companionship of the Holy Ghost.

President Lorenzo Snow taught that it is the "grand privilege of every Latter-day Saint . . . to have the manifestation of the spirit every day in our lives . . . [so] that we may know the light, and not be groveling continually in the dark."[4] The Holy Ghost will help us navigate our way through the darkness, and we should strive to have that Spirit with us daily. Moreover, the Holy Ghost will help us dispel doubt and uncertainty, and see the peace and the light that is necessary to make significant decisions.

In our modern era, Sister Sheri Dew explained, "This Church is a church of revelation. Our challenge is not one of getting the Lord to speak to us. Our challenge is hearing what he has to say."[5] Significant revelations are not merely for prophets and apostles only. Each member of the Church can be fortunate to receive daily, regular manifestations from the Holy Ghost. President Joseph F. Smith explained:

> It is the right and privilege of every man, every woman, and every child who has reached the years of accountability, to enjoy the spirit of revelation, to be possessed of the spirit of inspiration… It is the privilege of every individual member of the Church to have revelation for his own guidance, for the direction of his life and conduct.[6]

Unfortunately, when it comes to having the Spirit direct our lives, both temporally and spiritually, Brigham Young taught, "We live far beneath our privileges."[7] Indeed, too many of us are not guided by the Spirit as we should be. The Lord wants to reveal His will to us. It is our responsibility to discover during

---

4. Lorenzo Snow, *Conference Report*, April 1899. 52.
5. Sheri Dew, *No Doubt About It* (Salt Lake City: Bookcraft, 2001), 110.
6. Joseph F. Smith, *Gospel Doctrine*, 34.
7. Brigham Young, *Discourses of Brigham Young*, 32.

the course of our lives how the Holy Ghost speaks to us. And since revelation can come to all of us in many different ways, we should readily learn about those manifestations.

Different Manifestations of the Spirit

Our task is to listen and come to understand how the Spirit speaks to us specifically as individuals. Each of us can be touched and moved by the Spirit differently. Some will receive powerful manifestations, while for others, the Spirit can be more subtle. Other individuals could experience the Spirit through their thoughts and ideas, while for others, the Spirit speaks through feelings and emotions. Here are some different ways the Spirit can speak to us:

- The Spirit speaks as a soft voice (see D&C 85:6–7; 1 Samuel 3:1–10; 1 Kings 19:12).
- The Spirit can cause our hearts to burn (see 3 Nephi 11:3; Luke 24:32; D&C 9:6–9).
- The Spirit helps us to feel joy, peace, and hope (Galatians 5:22–23).
- The Spirit gives ideas to our mind and feelings to our hearts (D&C 8:2–3; Job 32:8).
- The Spirit occupies our mind and presses our feelings (see D&C 128:1).
- The Spirit can speak to us through the scriptures (see Joseph Smith—History 1:11–12).
- The Spirit constrains or warns us (see Alma 14:11).
- The Spirit gives us good feelings when something is right (see D&C 9:8–9; D&C 11:12; 1 Nephi 4:6).
- The Spirit enlightens our minds (see Alma 32:28; D&C 11:13).
- The Spirit leads us to do good (D&C 11:12).
- The Spirit gives feelings of peace and comfort (see John 14:27; Galatians 5:22; D&C 6:23).

- The Spirit instructs us and informs what we should do (see 2 Nephi 32:1–5).
- The Spirit comes as the Lord's voice (Enos 1:10).
- The Spirit gives comfort (D&C 88:3).
- The Spirit may inspire others to help us (D&C 46:29).
- The Spirt can bring all things to our remembrance (John 14:26).

This list is not all-inclusive. There are perhaps other ways the Spirit can be manifest. Nevertheless, our task is to be worthy so that we can receive revelations daily (see Helaman 11:23). Elder David A. Bednar taught:

> As we gain experience with the Holy Ghost, we learn that the intensity with which we feel the Spirit's influence is not always the same. Strong, dramatic spiritual impressions do not come to us frequently. Even as we strive to be faithful and obedient, there simply are times when the direction, assurance, and peace of the Spirit are not readily recognizable in our lives... the Spirit of the Lord usually communicates with us in ways that are quiet, delicate, and subtle.[8]

Once again, dramatic, powerful spiritual manifestations are rare. Elder Bednar is clear—the Spirit will speak to us most often in quiet, subtle ways. Over time, we can learn specifically how the Spirit speaks to us. As you navigate your way through the marriage decision, recognize that the Spirit can speak to you in different ways, in different places, and on different occasions. Pay close attention to your thoughts and feelings. Remember that the Spirit is often quiet and soft—not loud or harsh.

---

8. David A. Bednar, "That We May Always Have His Spirit to Be with Us," *Ensign*, May 2006.

Becoming Spiritually In Tune

In order for the Lord to speak to us through the Holy Ghost, we have to be worthy and in tune. We should repent daily so that we can always have the Spirit with us. We should strive to be obedient to the commandments, and strip ourselves of pride, envy, and selfishness. We should create a spiritual environment around us, with clean and wholesome surroundings. One helpful way to feel the Spirit in our lives is to listen to good music that invites the Spirit. We should also study the scriptures each day and listen to the words of our modern prophets and apostles. Although we cannot force the Spirit to speak to us, we can create an environment where the Spirit will feel comfortable attending. Brother Gerald N. Lund recommended the following process. He stated, "Sometimes we must deliberately put aside the cares of the world, put aside the rush of our daily lives, and find a quiet place and a quiet time where we can sit and ponder and reflect and mediate—and listen for that still small voice that whispers."[9]

Find moments in your life, especially as you make the marriage decision, to listen to some soft, instrumental music. Clear your head, and visualize what your Heavenly Father must look like. Imagine Him smiling at you as you address Him. Consider His love and concern for you. Pour out your heart to Him just as you would your dearest, closest friend. Finally, learn to listen. Instead of getting up off your knees directly after you say, "Amen," learn to stay in that kneeling position for a while and listen to your Heavenly Father. You may want to have a paper and pen nearby because He will speak to you. He will heal you, comfort you, and address your needs and concerns.

We worship a God that will answer our prayers. Many years ago, a member of the presiding bishopric, Bishop H. Burke

---

9. Gerald N. Lund, "The Voice of the Lord," *Brigham Young University Speeches*, 2 December 1997.

Petersen, made this promise to the students of Brigham Young University: "I want you to know that I know that whenever one of Heavenly Father's children kneels and talks to Him, He listens to each one. I know this as well as I know anything in this world—that Heavenly Father listens to every prayer from His children. I know our prayers ascend to heaven. Not matter what we may have done wrong, He listens to us."[10]

This statement from one of the Lord's servants has always given me the strength and confidence to pray and understand that our prayers will be answered. Be prepared to act on the revelation our Father in Heaven gives to you. By acting, He will give you more revelation over the course of your life.

Thought Questions:

1. How does the Holy Ghost usually speak to you?
2. How can you become more attuned to receiving answers from the Holy Ghost?

---

10. H. Burke Peterson, "Prayer: Try Again," *Brigham Young University Speeches*, 2 March 1980; https://speeches.byu.edu/talks/h-burke-peterson/prayer-try/

5

What is the relationship between making our own choices and being directed by the Spirit?

In the summer of 1981, I was attending a family home evening as a non-member in Pecos, Texas. I had just graduated from high school, and I was in West Texas working in the oil fields, earning as much money as I could before I began my first year of college. I had been investigating the Church since the tenth grade, and I assumed that Pecos would be the perfect place to continue my journey toward baptism. My anti-Mormon parents were back home in the suburbs of Houston, almost six hundred miles away. Presumably, I would be freed from hearing their negative comments about the Church. But I was also far away from my LDS high school friends who had been so instrumental in my gradual conversion to that point. If I was going to become a member of the Church, I wanted it to be my decision, and I did not want to be influenced by anyone else—not even my very best LDS friends.

During that family home evening on a cattle ranch on the outskirts of town, the father of the family, Brother Petersen, gave me some wise counsel. He asked me if I knew or believed that The Church of Jesus Christ of Latter-day Saints was the true Church. I said that I felt that I was getting close to believing that. He then counseled, "Do not ask the Lord if The Church of Jesus Christ of Latter-day Saints is the true church. Instead, in your prayer, tell the Lord that you know this church is true, and He will confirm that to you." Brother Petersen instructed me that the Lord wanted me to make that decision, and then I should present my decision to Him for a confirmation. Of course, as a non-member of the Church, I had never been taught such a concept before, but it sounded right to me.

That night, I went home to my rented apartment. At 10:00 p.m. I knelt down in the front yard, with no one else around. I told my Heavenly Father that I knew that The Church of Jesus Christ of Latter-day Saints was true. I then said in my prayer, "Heavenly Father, I know this, but can you confirm it to me? How do you feel about The Church of Jesus Christ of Latter-day Saints?" As you might guess, our Father in Heaven has strong feelings about His Church and His gospel. Immediately, I felt the most powerful experience of the Spirit that I ever felt in my life to that point. Literally, that prevailing feeling went through the top of my head and slowly moved down to the tips of my toes. I'm much older now than I was then. If that spiritual experience happened today, tears would come very easily. But in those days, there was nothing but utter delight and happiness. I remember smiling from ear to ear. I do not think I had ever been happier. When I got up off my knees, I knew for sure that The Church of Jesus Christ of Latter-day Saints was God's true church on the earth. Consequently, I was baptized a week or two later, and as they say, the rest is history.

For you, the same principles can apply. Brother Peterson's counsel was wise and helpful. Learn to gather the information, analyze the date, make your own decision, and then present that decision to the Lord. The Lord wants us to solve our own problems and then counsel with Him in prayer "and receive a spiritual confirmation that our decisions are correct."[1] The Lord loves effort, and He certainly will honor you for doing your homework before you pray to Him for counsel and guidance.

---

1. Bruce R. McConkie, *Ensign*, January 1976, 11.

Agency and Inspiration

We have come to this earth to learn, grow, experience challenges, develop faith, receive the essential ordinances of the gospel, and believe it or not, make decisions.[2] The Lord wants us to decide things. We need to decide to decide. He has provided the means for us to make decisions. He has given us many resources, such as parents, friends, and Church leaders. Our Father in Heaven has provided us with patriarchal blessings, the scriptures, the words of the prophets, and of course, the Holy Ghost. He has given us many tools to make decisions correctly. Therefore, seek advice from the mentors around you. How do they feel about your marriage decision? How do they feel about your potential partner? What have modern prophets said about the marriage decision? Have you searched for their statements and messages on selecting an eternal companion? What counsel does your patriarchal blessing provide on receiving revelation, and what does it say about the person you desire to marry?

Years ago, Dr. J. Bonner Ritchie spoke in a Brigham Young University devotional. He taught, "Revelations don't just follow questions, they follow proposals. They follow proactive behavior on the part of individuals who care enough to study, who care enough to trust, and who care enough to formulate proposals."[3] Indeed, the Lord wants us to use our own agency to make decisions, or proposals, and then to present those decisions to the Lord for a confirmation.

A classic example of this principle occurred in the book of Ether. You may remember that the Jaredites were to build barges to cross the ocean on their way to the promised land. However, in chapter 2, there were two major challenges regarding the barges that would

---

2. See Mark D. Ogletree, *Preparing for Your Celestial Marriage* (American Fork, Utah: Covenant Communications, 2017), 188–190.
3. J. Bonner Ritchie, "Taking Sweet Counsel," *Brigham Young University Speeches*, 25 June 1991; https://speeches.byu.edu/talks/j-bonner-ritchie/taking-sweet-counsel/

need to be resolved. First, there was no light, and second, there was no air (see Ether 2:18–19). Talk about a claustrophobic nightmare. In some cases, the Lord speaks to His children directly, without any proposals. Therefore, in the case of the air problem, the Lord provided very specific instruction on what to do. I will not go into those details, but suffice it to say, the Lord solved that problem promptly. Sometimes we forget that almost immediately, the brother of Jared did exactly as the Lord commanded him, making holes in the tops and bottoms of those vessels.

However, once the "air" problem was solved, the brother of Jared still recognized that there was no light in the barges (see Ether 2:22). Instead of instructing the brother of Jared on how to resolve that problem as He did with the "air" issue, the Lord asked, "What will ye that I should do that ye may have light in your vessels?" (Ether 2:24). Or, in other words, the Lord wanted the brother of Jared to solve this problem on his own. Simply put, He wanted the brother of Jared to make a proposal, or a decision. Consequently, the brother of Jared decided to go up to the Mount Shelem, where he found sixteen smooth stones, and brought them to the Lord, asking Him to touch them (see Ether 3:1–4). The Lord touched those stones, and they provided light to the vessels (see Ether 6:2). As with the brother of Jared, many times in our own lives, the Lord wants us to solve our own problems and make our own decisions.

Elder Bruce R. McConkie once explained,

> It is not, never has been, and never will be the design and purpose of the Lord—however much we seek him in prayer—to answer all our problems and concerns without struggle and effort on our part. This mortality is a probationary estate. In it we have our agency. We are being tested to see how we will respond in various situations; how we will decide issues; what course we will pursue while we are here walking, not by sight, but by faith. Hence, we are to solve our own problems and then to counsel

with the Lord in prayer and receive a spiritual confirmation that our decisions are correct.[4]

I love that the Lord trusts us and wants us to make major life decisions. He will give us the guidance and the direction we need, but He wants us to do our homework. We are to use both agency and prayer. However, we can begin with the intelligence, knowledge, and experience the Lord has provided us to solve our problems. In another setting, Elder Bruce R. McConkie gave more specific counsel on this subject. He taught the students at Brigham Young University that if they wanted to marry, they should follow this procedure:

> You go to work, you use the agency and power and ability that God has given you. You use every faculty and get all the judgment you can center on the problem, you make up your own mind and then, to be sure that you don't err, you counsel with the Lord. You talk it over. You say, "I know what I think; what do you think?" And if you get the calm sweet surety that comes from the Holy Spirit, you know you've reached the right conclusion.[5]

Therefore, gather all of the information you can regarding the marriage decision. For every decision we make, first, we are to study things out in our minds. Then, we are to ask the Lord if it is right (see Doctrine and Covenants 9:8). Therefore, talk to your friends, counsel with Church leaders, and visit with your parents. See your potential spouse in a variety of situations. Spend time with each other and engage in meaningful activities. Ultimately, you will need to make a decision regarding marriage. Once you have made your choice, present that decision to the Lord, and He will confirm it to you if it is right. That confirmation may

---

4. McConkie, "Why the Lord Ordained Prayer," *Ensign*, Jan. 1976, 11.
5. McConkie, "Agency or Inspiration," *Brigham Young University Speeches of the Year*, 1972-1973, 115–116.

not always come immediately, like while you are praying, or even shortly thereafter. Sometimes the confirmation can come when you least expect it, like when you are driving in your car, walking down the sidewalk, or studying for an exam. The confirmation can certainly come while sitting in a church meeting or while attending the temple. Know and understand that these confirmations can come many times. Answers from the Lord do not often come in a one-time grand fashion. Instead, answers come multiple times and often in a myriad of ways.

I recommend that you seek the Lord's inspiration many times during the dating and courtship process. Make a decision, and present it to the Lord. Your prayer may look something like this: "Heavenly Father, as you know, I have been dating _____ for several months now. She is spiritual, she is smart, she is happy, she is capable, and I am very attracted to her. I believe she will be a wonderful mother, leader, and friend. I know that the gospel is the most important thing in her life. I deeply desire to be with her for the rest of my life. I feel strongly that she should be my wife, not only for this life but for the eternities. Wilt thou help me to know that this is the right decision for me? Please help me to feel thy confirming Spirit."

You do not need to say this exact prayer, but at least this is a start. My example here may prompt you as to what your specific prayer could look like. So, if you are ready, make the marriage decision. Present your proposal or your decision to the Lord, and He will let you know, through the Spirit, if what you have decided is correct and aligns with His will.

Thought Questions

1. What are some of the bad decisions you have made in your life? Did you present these decisions to the Lord?
2. If you are in a serious relationship right now, what are some of the "common sense" indicators that you should marry this person?

6

How does the Holy Ghost work through our thoughts?

When it comes to receiving revelation regarding the marriage decision, understandably most individuals are seeking spiritual manifestations of epic proportions. Perhaps some are looking for a Pentecostal experience, complete with heavenly messengers and angelic choirs. Many individuals suppose that such a magnificent revelation would prevent them from making the wrong decision, and certainly help them to know without a doubt that they have found their true eternal companion. Nevertheless, many are surprised to learn that revelation most often comes in less dramatic ways.

Unfortunately, many Latter-day Saints discount the subtle thoughts and ideas that they experience, perhaps feeling that personal revelation should be more intense, and on a grander scale.[1] Many years ago, President Spencer W. Kimball provided this counsel:

> Many people of our own day expect that revelations will come only in spectacular vision on Sinais accompanied

---

1. See Mark D. Ogletree, *Preparing for Your Celestial Marriage* (American Fork, Utah: Covenant Communications, 2017), 195–96.

with lightnings and thunderings. . . . Even in our day, many people . . . expect if there be revelation it will come with awe-inspiring, earth-shaking display. . . .

The burning bushes, the smoking mountains, the sheets of four-footed beasts, the Cumorahs, and the Kirtlands were realities; but they were the exceptions. The great volume of revelation came to Moses and to Joseph and comes to today's prophet in the less spectacular way—that of deep impressions, without spectacle or glamour or dramatic events. Always expecting the spectacular, many will miss entirely the constant flow of revealed communication.[2]

Face it—we feel that grand decisions should be accompanied by grand revelations. When it comes to receiving a spiritual answer regarding marriage, we want at least an angelic choir or heavenly messengers playing their trumpets on top of the temple. Perhaps a visit from our deceased grandfather would be the least that our Heavenly Father could do when it comes to strong and powerful revelations.

Over the years, I have informally polled the married students in my classes, asking them to explain the "type" of revelation they received while making the marriage decision. In most cases, they explain that the revelation process was plain and simple, usually consisting of thoughts and ideas that entered their minds. These students expressed that they had come to understand that such thoughts and ideas were revelation—a direct answer to their prayers—although they had been taught that revelation was supposed to be more dramatic and spectacular.

In Doctrine and Covenants 8:2, we learn that revelation can come as thoughts to our mind. President David O. McKay stated that for active and faithful members of the Church, the Holy Ghost will normally speak to them through their thoughts

---

2. Spencer W. Kimball, *Germany Area Conference*, August 1973, 76–77.

or their conscience.[3] That means that for most of us who are active and faithful in the Church, striving to do our best, the Holy Ghost will speak to us as thoughts to our mind. Similarly, Joseph Smith, explained that "a person may profit by noticing the first intimation of the spirit of revelation; for instance, when you feel *pure intelligence* flowing into you, it may give you *sudden strokes of ideas*, so that by noticing it, you may find it fulfilled the same day of soon; (i.e.) those things that were presented unto your minds by the Spirit of God, will come to pass."[4]

Like President McKay's idea, the Prophet Joseph is reminding us how sacred and instrumental our thoughts can be when it comes to making decisions. Indeed, many of the thoughts, ideas, and perhaps intelligence flowing into our minds comes directly from heaven. As a bishop, it was not unusual for me to sit on the stand in sacrament meeting, look across the congregation, and have clear thoughts enter my mind, such as the following:

- "I need to text Ken about this week's youth activity."
- "I do not see Spencer here today. I need to check up on him."
- "I need to visit Sister Brown today. She looks like she's having a tough day."
- "We need to instruct our young men on some issues regarding the sacrament."

Such thoughts seemed to come to me continually—not just while I sat on the stand—but during most days. These thoughts were so continuous that I later told someone that the thing I would miss the most about being a bishop was the constant flow of revelation. Do not discount the thoughts and ideas that come to your mind, especially when they inspire you to do something good or worthwhile such as marrying in the temple.

---

3. David O. McKay, as cited in Stephen R. Covey, *The Divine Center*, 180.
4. Joseph Smith, *Teachings of the Prophet Joseph Smith*, 151; emphasis added.

While dating Janie, I had many thoughts about her and our potential future. When I asked our Father in Heaven about marrying her, thoughts filled my mind such as, "Yes, by all means," or even "Of course." One day I went to the Provo temple, expecting a grandiose manifestation. I fully anticipated my deceased father or at least some other angel to appear to me and give me instructions on what I should do. However, as I sat in the celestial room and prayed over the matter, I had a clear thought: "You would be really stupid if you didn't marry Janie." That was all. Although I wanted more, I recognized that message in the temple was all that I needed. Of course, I hoped that she would receive a similar revelation.

Unfortunately, too many of us do not trust our thoughts. We often question, "Are those my thoughts and ideas, or do they come from the Spirit?" I once heard Elder David A. Bednar explain that everything that is good comes from God (see Moroni 7:12). In fact, we learn in the Book of Mormon that the things of God invite us and inspire us to do good continually, and everything that invites us and entices us to do good, love God, and serve Him is inspired of God (see Moroni 7:13). Therefore, if we feel inspired or driven to do something good, then it comes from God.[5] If the Holy Ghost is our constant companion, and we are living the gospel of Jesus Christ, we should trust that the thoughts we have, especially the good ones, are from God.

If you are having thoughts to marry the person of your dreams in the holy temple, then act on those thoughts. Trust that your thoughts are coming from God, and follow those thoughts toward the temple. Write those thoughts down in your journal, and you will discover, over time, that these thoughts will sync together well with the other thoughts you have experienced. In

---

5. David A. Bednar and Sister Susan Bednar, "How Can I Recognize Revelation," *Face to Face*, 26 January 2016; https://www.youtube.com/watch?v=2_EzSp84wbA

fact, these recorded thoughts can provide a unifying message of faith, hope, and direction. The thoughts you experience as you make the marriage decision can become the greatest source of your personal revelation.

Thought Questions

1. Can you recall revelations you have received throughout your life as thoughts to your mind? What were they?
2. Have you ever had an idea or a thought come to you that you knew was from God because you could not have come up with that idea on your own? What was it?

7

How does the Holy Ghost work through our feelings?

Throughout my life—and I am sure throughout your lives—I have felt strong *feelings* from the Holy Ghost. In family stories, in testimonies, and in religious classrooms, experiences have been shared, which begin with phrases such as:

- "I *felt* that I needed to call you."
- "I had a *feeling* to speak to the person I was sitting next to on the airplane."
- "I *sensed* that I should turn down the second street instead of the first one."

Consider the following example. For almost ten years, we lived in Mesa, Arizona. Every Christmas during that period, we traveled to Janie's home in Houston. I was in graduate school during most of that time and worked full-time. Nevertheless, funds were always tight, so we never flew. In case you have never driven from Mesa to Houston, I promise you that there is not much to see, other than desert for about a thousand miles.

On one particular drive, we were in West Texas, traveling down Interstate 10. We were methodically making our way across a very boring stretch of highway. To make matters worse, our two young children were very fussy. They had already been in their car seats for a full day and were completely "done." And since they were "done," Janie and I were "done" too. As our children were crying, I noticed a hitchhiker walking on the side of the highway. Although I am not the kind of person who picks up hitchhikers, I had a strong feeling come over me, compelling me to pull over to offer him a ride. Even Janie, who is the calmest person I know, was a bit troubled that I was going to pick up a hitchhiker. But once again, I had a strong feeling to do so, and I acted.

We pulled over to the shoulder of the highway, and I began to converse with the "Christmas Hitchhiker." I learned that his car had broken down a few miles back, and he simply needed to get to the next town to hire a tow truck driver so that they could go and pick up his car. I told him we would be happy to give him a ride to the next town, which was probably about fifty miles down the highway. He related to us that he had been trying to get help for hours, but no one would stop.

The first miracle is that he sat between our two fussy babies in the back seat. Our children were so petrified that they instantly quit crying and just looked straight ahead. They were completely paralyzed with fear. In our conversation, we learned the hitchhiker was a nice man who worked on an offshore oil well. He was so grateful for us giving him a ride that when we dropped him off, he gave us several hundred dollars. Of course, Janie refused to accept the money, but the hitchhiker insisted, and I gladly took the money. That was the second miracle!

Now, here's why. We were so poor in those days that we literally had no money to pull off Christmas that year. Our only option was to go shopping once we arrived in Houston and purchase most of our children's Christmas gifts with a credit card. However, with the money from the hitchhiker, we were able to provide Christmas for our children without going into any debt. We were full tithe payers, and I viewed this as both a tithing and a Christmas miracle.

There have been other times in my life when I had similar feelings but did not act. On another occasion, I was driving to work and noticed an older woman pulled off the side of the road, with the hood of her car up. Obviously, her car had broken down, but I knew if I stopped to help her, I would be late to work. I was teaching professionally at the time, and arriving late to your own classroom is not acceptable. I wrestled with my feelings and decided that surely another good Samaritan could help. However, with each mile I drove to work, the guiltier I felt. Finally, I arrived at work and walked into my classroom. I explained to my students that I had to go back and help this old woman. So, I left and drove back to where her car had broken down. But she was nowhere to be found. Either someone had helped her, or she was one of the Three Nephites and probably did not need my help anyway. Nevertheless, I could not help but feel chastened by the Lord for not responding to that strong feeling.

I am sure many of you have had similar experiences of feeling strongly about something but not acting on those feelings. C. S. Lewis wrote, "The more often he feels without acting, the less he will be able to act, and, in the long run, the less he will be able to feel."[1] I have always been haunted by these words. By *not* responding to the feelings of the Spirit, the Lord will most likely trust us less and therefore, give us less. I do not like that idea. This statement has been a reminder to treasure every spiritual prompting that I feel and then to act as directed.

Doctrinal Underpinnings of Spiritual Feelings

Many years ago, Bishop H. Burke Peterson explained, "Most answers from the Lord are felt in our heart as a warm, comfortable

---

1. C.S. Lewis, *The Screwtape Letters* (New York: Harper-Collins Publishers, 1996), 66–67.

expression, or they may come as thoughts to our mind. They come to those who are prepared and who are patient."[2] Similarly, in the Doctrine and Covenants, the Lord instructed, "I will tell you in your mind and in your heart, by the Holy Ghost, which shall come upon you and which shall dwell in your heart" (Doctrine and Covenants 8:2). Yes, the Lord will reveal things to our minds but also our hearts. He often reveals things to our hearts through our feelings. The heart is the epicenter of our feelings and our emotions.

President Ezra Taft Benson taught:

> We hear the words of the Lord most often by a feeling. If we are humble and sensitive, the Lord will prompt us through our feelings. That is why spiritual promptings move us on occasion to great joy, sometimes to tears. Many times my emotions have been made tender and my feelings very sensitive when touched by the Holy Spirit. The Holy Ghost causes our feelings to be more tender.[3]

When it comes to making the marriage decision, do not discount the feelings you are experiencing. President Boyd K. Packer taught, "Perhaps the greatest single thing I learned from reading the Book of Mormon is that the voice of the Spirit comes as a *feeling* rather than a sound. You will learn, as I have learned, to 'listen' for that voice that is *felt* rather than *heard*. . . . It is a spiritual voice that comes into the mind as a thought or a feeling put into your heart."[4] As you prepare for marriage, pay attention to your feelings, especially those feelings that are directing you to marriage. Many of you will begin to have deep feelings for the

---

2. H. Burke Peterson, *Conference Report*, October 1973, 13.
3. Ezra Taft Benson, *Come Unto Christ*, 20.
4. Boyd K. Packer, "Counsel to Youth," *Ensign*, November 2011, 17–18; emphasis in original.

person you are to marry but also deep feelings from the Spirit confirming that what you are doing is right.

During the bleak winter months of 1846–1847, many of the Saints were starving and freezing at temporary stopping locations such as Winter Quarters. Brigham Young, as the President of the Quorum of the Twelve, was leading the exodus across the plains, and he needed counsel. On several occasions, the Prophet Joseph Smith appeared to him, providing direction, comfort, and assistance. On one such occasion, Joseph told Brigham the following:

> Tell the people to be humble and faithful, and be sure to keep the spirit of the Lord and it will lead them right. Be careful and not turn away the still small voice; it will teach you what to do and where to go; it will yield the fruits of the kingdom. Tell the brethren to keep their hearts open to conviction, so that when the Holy Ghost comes to them, their hearts will be ready to receive it. They can tell the Spirit of the Lord from all other spirits; it will whisper peace and joy to their souls; it will take malice, hatred, strife and all evils from their hearts, and their whole desire will be to do good. . . . Tell the Brethren if they will follow the spirit of the Lord they will go right. Be sure to tell the people to keep the Spirit of the Lord.[5]

Notice how many times in this statement Joseph mentioned the word "heart," which is indicative of "feelings." He also mentioned the words "peace" and "joy." Feelings of peace are so important to understand that I have devoted a full chapter to that concept in this book. However, feelings of joy also deserve our full consideration.

---

5. Eden Watson, *Manuscript History of Brigham Young* (Salt Lake City: E.J. Watson, 1971), 529–531; as cited by Elder Marion G. Romney, *Conference Report*, April 1944, 140–141.

King Benjamin called our attention to the connection between the Spirit of the Lord and joy when he taught, "He has *poured out his Spirit upon you*, and has caused that your hearts should be *filled with joy*, and has caused that your mouths should be stopped that ye could not find utterance, so exceeding *great was your joy*" (Mosiah 4:20; emphasis added). Likewise, in the Doctrine and Covenants, the Lord taught, "I will impart unto you of *my Spirit*, which shall enlighten your mind, which shall *fill your soul with joy*" (Doctrine and Covenants 11:13; emphasis added). There is an incredible connection between the Spirit of the Lord and joy. Joy is certainly a key indicator of the Spirit.

Feelings of Joy and Happiness

As you engage in making the marriage decision, focus on feelings of joy and happiness that can be manifest to you on many occasions. I remember when Janie and were dating seriously, I felt so happy. I was in love for sure, and the prospect of being married to her for time and all eternity brought happiness to me on many occasions. I hope that she experienced similar feelings. Otherwise, I would feel bad that I have been having so much fun by myself.

Dating, courtship, and engagement should bring joy and happiness to your heart. That does not mean that you will not have problems, because you will, and that does not mean that you will not occasionally disagree or have to work your way through some issues, because you will have to do that too. However, overall, you should be happy and excited. Joy should fill your hearts as you contemplate being married and being together for the rest of your mortal days, and for eternity.

Several years ago, one of our children was in a serious relationship, and it looked like they were heading toward marriage. However, there were several red flags that caught our attention as parents. Perhaps the most significant was that our child did not seem particularly happy. It was almost as if they were planning to "go and get married" like many of us have to "go to the dentist and get a root canal." I did not sense the happiness, elation, or joy. After all, the prospect of being married to your best friend should cause you to practically leap for joy and excitement.

I approached my daughter on this issue, and after presenting several of my concerns about her relationship with this young man, I said, "Convince me that you are happy and elated about marrying this person, because I do not feel that you are." My daughter's response did not persuade me that she was happy, and I told her that she should reconsider the prospect of marriage. Fortunately, she did just that, and within another year, she and her former boyfriend were both happily married to other individuals.

The Apostle Paul taught that fruits of the Spirit include love, joy, peace, and several other attributes, including gentleness, goodness, and meekness (see Galatians 5:22–23). Joy as an attribute of the Spirit cannot be overemphasized. When we feel the Spirit in our lives, we often feel happy, joyful, exuberant, and cheerful. Look for those feelings and identify them as you approach the marriage decision.

Thought Questions

1. Do you feel joy and happiness in your current relationship? How so?
2. Do others—your friends and family— perceive that you are happy in this relationship?

8

How can peace be a manifestation of the Spirit?

Many years ago, I read a story in the *Ensign* that has remained with me. Brother Jay E. Jensen related the experience when his one-year-old daughter contracted viral meningitis. After the devastating diagnosis, the doctor explained to Brother and Sister Jensen that they would know within the next twenty-four hours if their baby daughter would live or die. The Jensens fasted and prayed for her recovery. Even so, the baby lingered near death for a week—much longer than the doctor had predicted. Toward the end of the week, the Jensen's fasted again—this time with their ward members. When they prayed, they expressed to their Father in Heaven "Thy will be done." Elder Jensen reported, "A peace as tangible and real as anything we ever have experienced came to our minds. We were not in turmoil, nor were we anxious about the matter. We did not know whether she would live or die, but we were at peace. Happily, she began to recover."[1]

Feelings of peace can often calm our troubled hearts and restore happiness and hope to our souls. President Ezra Taft Benson explained, "Though persecutions arise, though reverses come, in

---

1. Jay E. Jensen, "Have I Received An Answer from the Spirit?" *Ensign,* April 1989.

prayer we can find reassurance, for God will speak peace to the soul. That peace, that spirit of serenity, is life's greatest blessing."[2] Peace is one of life's most sought after gifts. In fact, peace can be a great blessing in your life, especially while praying over the marriage decision. As you seek answers from the Spirit, you may not feel a burning of the bosom, nor angels, nor trumpets, but perhaps you will be able to feel peaceful about your decision.

Synonyms for peace include harmony, calmness, tranquility, order, contentment, and even stability. Perhaps you have had experiences in your life where the Holy Ghost helped you to feel calm, peaceful, assured, and content. Such peace can comfort us in times of trial but also help us as we make big decisions in our lives—like the marriage decision. In some cases, you may not understand how your decision will work out, but look for the peace that can bring calm to your troubled or unsettled heart.

One author wrote, "Peace, prompted by the Spirit, is one of the most sublime among spiritual experiences. . . . There is no circumstance of comfort or place of leisure that can duplicate that peace provided by the Holy Spirit."[3]

In a revelation to Oliver Cowdery, the Lord exclaimed, "Did I not speak peace to your mind concerning the matter? What greater witness can you have than from God?" (Doctrine and Covenants 6:23). Feelings of peace can help us understand that the decision we have made is correct, that things will work out. Peace gives us the assurance that we are on the right path and that the Lord is with us.

Elder Gerald N. Lund explained,

> Feelings of peace are a common way the Spirit speaks to us. Whether we are struggling with a challenge, seeking strength

---

2. Ezra Taft Benson, *Ensign*, February 1990, 5.
3. Erroll R. Fish, *Promptings of the Spirit* (Mesa, Arizona: Cogent Publishing, 1990), 62.

to endure adversity, or searching for the answer to a vexing question, suddenly the turmoil and the uncertainty and the anxiety are replaced with a deep feeling of peace. Words cannot adequately described this feeling. But it permeates the soul and brings rest to a troubled heart.[4]

I have had significant challenges many times throughout my life. As I have prayed over those issues, I have felt the peace that the Savior offers—even though I still did not understand how everything would work out. I trusted the Lord and moved forward with faith. As you make the marriage decision, look for the peace that the Prince of Peace offers. Become aware of the feelings that provide assurance, contentment, and happiness. These feelings come from our Father in Heaven.

Practical Applications of Peace

Indeed, peace often comes to those who are in the midst of turmoil, challenge, or uncertainty. For example, when Janie and I were approaching marriage, I had no idea how we would make it financially, and I certainly did not know how we would pay for tuition when the fall semester rolled around. However, I felt at peace, and although I did not know how everything would work out, Janie and I trusted that everything was going to be okay. I am happy to report that, thirty-plus years later, things did work out. I have felt that same peace in my life when a child has been rushed to a hospital, when we have been faced with accepting a move to another state, or when the timing of some major events needed to align perfectly for a miracle to occur.

However, peace is not only for times of trauma and distress. Peace can also become a calming influence as we make

---

4. Gerald N. Lund, *Hearing the Voice of the Lord: Principles and Patterns of Personal Revelation* (Salt Lake City: Deseret Book, 2007), 94–95.

monumental decisions in our lives. For example, as you make the marriage decision, pay close attention to feelings of peace and happiness. If you cannot find any reason to question your decision, then be grateful for the peace you are feeling. Continue to move forward with faith. If the Lord needs to stop you, He will.

Years ago, I completed my doctoral degree at Utah State University. By the time I graduated, Janie and I had seven children; in fact, we almost had more children than we had dollars. Upon graduation, I was transferred by my company to the Dallas area. We were excited for that move because we were Texans, and in essence, we were going home. However, because of a dip in the housing market in Utah, we ended up selling our home in Cache Valley for a loss instead of a gain. To make matters worse, the economy in the Dallas area was booming, and we wondered how we would afford a home large enough for nine people.

Janie and I left our home in Utah and traveled down to the suburbs of Dallas one weekend to look for homes. It did not take long for us to become somewhat discouraged. Every home that we liked and believed would fit our needs was out of our price range. We also had the sad realization that we would not have as much money as we probably needed for a down payment.

Nevertheless, through a small miracle, we found the best possible home that would fit our needs. It was located in the wonderful suburb of McKinney, Texas—a place where many LDS people had gathered. Since the home wasn't built yet, we would be able to choose wall colors, carpet colors, light fixtures, and a few other options. Janie and I were excited because this would be our first brand new house after being married for fifteen years. Nevertheless, after crunching the numbers, I still did not know how we were going to make this work.

The following day we would need to make the decision and sign on the dotted line. I decided to go for a jog early that morning nearby our hotel. As I ran, I contemplated our decision about the house. We knew it felt right, but I still did not know how everything would work out financially. Then, I had an idea enter my mind from our prophet in those days—President Gordon B. Hinckley. The thought also happened to be the title of his biography: *Go Forward with Faith*. Instantly, I knew that we were to move forward with this house—we were to go forward with faith. As I concentrated on this principle, I felt a sense of complete peace and calmness come over me. I knew that the Lord was in our decision, and he wanted us to move into the house we had selected.

From that point on, I no longer worried if we would be able to make everything work financially. I knew all I needed to know. The Lord was in charge. He was telling me, "Go forward with faith," and so we did. Even though I did not understand how all of this would work, we took a step into the darkness.

Within a matter of months, we moved from Logan, Utah, to McKinney, Texas. Almost from the day we moved into our new home, our children began to thrive. They found wonderful friends who were strong members of the Church. They became successful academically and athletically; in fact, they made a huge difference at the high school and middle school they attended. Janie and I were able to develop lifelong friendships, raise our family in a wonderful environment, and serve in callings that we loved. Janie eventually became the Young Women president of that ward, and a few years after that, I became the bishop. There was no question in our minds that our home in McKinney, Texas, was the right place for us.

Even though we may not understand how things will work out, when we feel His peace, we need to trust Him. Instead of thinking of the fifty reasons something will not work out, we should focus on the five or six reasons that a particular decision will be a great blessing. Furthermore, when the decisions we make in our lives are correct, the Lord will help us feel peace—His peace—a peace that "passeth all understanding" (Philippians 4:7).

How to Obtain Peace

The Savior taught, "Learn of me, and listen to my words; walk in the meekness of my Spirit, and you shall have peace in me" (Doctrine and Covenants 19:23). It appears that this verse provides an answer regarding how to feel at peace with the marriage decision. First, learn of the Savior. Read the scriptures and the words of His living prophets. Study *His* life and teachings. Second, listen to *His* words. How can we do that? Perhaps by listening to the scriptures or general conference proceedings as we jog, walk, or ride in our cars. We should especially prepare ourselves to hear *Him* speaking to us through the Holy Ghost. Third, we are to walk in the meekness of *His* spirit. How do we do that? Keep an open mind. Do not assume that you know more than you do. Strip yourselves of pride. Let the Spirit coach you, teach you, and train you. As you are humble, the Lord will lead you by the hand and give you answers to your prayers (Doctrine and Covenants 112:10). This is the scriptural formula to experience peace in our lives, and to feel peace in the decisions we make.

Sister Barbara Thompson confirmed what these scriptures teach: "Most often personal revelation will come as we study the scriptures, listen to and follow the counsel of prophets and other Church leaders, and seek to live faithful, righteous lives."[5] Sister Thompson has provided a powerful formula for personal revelation. The Lord wants us to understand His will for us, and almost more than anything else, He wants to communicate with us.

Thought Questions

1. When was the last time you felt peace in answer to a prayer?
2. Have you felt peace with the marriage decision? How so?

---

5. Barbara Thompson, "Personal Revelation and Testimony," *Ensign*, November 2011.

9

Are you being prompted by the Holy Ghost or your own emotions?

President Howard W. Hunter exclaimed, "I get concerned when it appears that strong emotion or free-flowing tears are equated with the presence of the Spirit. Certainly the Spirt of the Lord can bring strong emotional feelings, including tears, but that outward manifestation ought not be confused with the presence of the Spirit itself."[1] Sometimes, it can be difficult to detect the difference between our own emotions and promptings from the Holy Ghost. During the dating and courtship phase, couples can be susceptible to powerful emotions that often accompany relationships. In fact, strong emotions can be brought to the surface by many sources, including close physical contact, deep conversations, spending inordinate amounts of time together, and even from dreaming of marriage.

Unfortunately, sometimes our own emotions can cloud our ability to feel the Holy Ghost. Many college students have told me over the years that it is often difficult for them to separate their feelings from spiritual manifestations. Elder Boyd K. Packer explained, "The spiritual part of us and the emotional

---

1. Howard W. Hunter, "Eternal Investments," *Address given to CES Personnel*, 10 February 1989, Salt Lake City, 3.

part of us are so closely linked that [it is] possible to mistake an emotional impulse for something spiritual. We occasionally find people who receive what they assume to be spiritual promptings from God, when those promptings are either centered in the emotions or are from the adversary."[2]

As I reflect on my life, I recognize that several times I became wrapped up in the emotions of a potential decision and consequently was not guided by the Spirit. For example, once I introduced one of my daughters to a young man whom I thought was quite outstanding. I was impressed by this returned missionary on many different levels, and I became emotionally caught up in the desire for my daughter to date him. Looking back on this experience, I realize that my decision was not directed by the Holy Ghost. This young man ended up being very different from whom I thought he was. Because I became caught up in the emotions of the situation, I was quite misled. My daughter broke off their relationship after a few short months. Today, she is happily married to someone else.

Elder Richard G. Scott taught, "The inspiring influence of the Holy Ghost can be overcome or masked by strong emotions, such as anger, hate, passion, fear, or pride. . . . Strong emotions overcome the delicate promptings of the Holy Spirit."[3] This is why we must be careful. Love, and even lust, are accompanied by strong emotions, and sometimes we can become misled. Dr. Ned Hill, who is the former dean of the Brigham Young University Marriot School of Management, spoke at a Brigham Young University–Idaho devotional several years ago. Dr. Hill stated, "I suspect we sometimes may be confused because the Spirit's voice often touches our emotions—sometimes very powerfully. However, not all strongly felt emotions are the voice of the Spirit. Sometimes our fears, our excitement, our pride, our

---

2. Boyd K. Packer, "The Candle of the Lord," *Ensign*, January 1983.
3. Richard G. Scott, "To Acquire Spiritual Guidance," *Ensign*, November 2009.

greed, our feelings of infatuation may be construed as promptings of the Spirit."[4]

These emotions can sometimes prod us *toward* the marriage altar or can *scare* us away from it. Emotions can often be tricky to navigate. Perhaps some of the feelings Latter-day Saints receive are actually what Dr. Carlfred Broderick called "hormonal revelations,"[5] meaning that hormones, rather than spiritual manifestations, are driving a couple toward the marriage altar. We must be able to discern between what is "hormonal" and what is "spiritual," to say the least!

The obvious question is, "How can you tell the difference from a prompting of the Spirit and your own powerful emotions?" Here are some keys to ponder:

1. Consider the law of multiple witnesses. If the revelation is true, then it will be revealed to you and your partner, multiple times, in perhaps multiple ways, such as thoughts, ideas, common sense, and feelings. Remember that the fruits of the Spirit include love, joy, peace, longsuffering, gentleness, goodness, faith, meekness, and temperance (see Galatians 5:22–23). If the revelation you receive is of God, then you will also experience some of these feelings—especially peace and joy. Remember, there is no greater witness from the Holy Ghost than peace (see D&C 6:23).
2. Does the inspiration you are receiving square with gospel principles and eternal truths? For instance, are there gospel principles in conflict with your revelation, such as agency, happiness, joy, or even worthiness? On the other hand, does your inspiration align with the gospel of Jesus

---

4. Ned C. Hill, "Hearing the Voice of the Spirit," Brigham Young University–Idaho Devotional, "Hearing the Voice of the Spirit, 11 March 2008.
5. See Carlfred Broderick, *One Flesh, One Heart: Putting Celestial Love into Your Temple Marriage* (Salt Lake City: Deseret Book, 1986), 21.

Christ? Does your revelation inspire you to be a better person, keep your covenants, and serve and bless others?
3. Does the revelation you are receiving square with good common sense? Elder Boyd K. Packer asked, "How can you know if a prompting is an inspiration or a temptation? My answer to that must surely expose my great confidence in young people. I believe young people, when properly taught, are basically sensible. In the Church we are not exempt from common sense. You can know to begin with that you won't be prompted from any righteous source to steal, to lie, to cheat, to join anyone in any kind of moral transgression. . . . Your conscience] will prompt you to know the things that are wrong. Don't smother it. . . . If ever you are confused and feel that you are being misled, go for counsel to your parents, and to your leaders."[6] What does your common sense tell you? Does the revelation you have received align with your common sense?
4. Does the spiritual manifestation you have received inspire you to do something good? Are you feeling strongly that you need to marry a wonderful person in the holy temple? In the book of Moroni, we are given a grand key: "Everything which inviteth to do good, and to persuade to believe in Christ, is sent forth by the power and gift of Christ; wherefore ye may know with a perfect knowledge it is of God. But whatsoever thing persuadeth men to do evil, and believe not in Christ, and deny him, and serve not God, then ye may know with a perfect knowledge it is of the devil; for after this manner doth the devil work, for he persuadeth no man to do good, no, not one" (Moroni 7:16–18). If the inspiration you are receiving is directing you to do something good, then it is of God.

---

6. Boyd K. Packer, "Prayers and Answers," *Ensign*, November 1979, 19.

Moreover, if your revelation is in harmony with the plan of salvation, the commandments, and covenants, then you can know you are on solid ground.

5. Does the revelation you have received edify both you and your future spouse? To edify is to improve, build, and uplift. Does the revelation you have received inspire you to be better? If the revelation you are experiencing is true, it will be manifest to both you and your future spouse. In the Doctrine and Covenants, we learn that if a revelation is of God, then "both are edified and rejoice together" (D&C 50:22). However, if the message you have received does not edify, then it is not of God (see D&C 50:23).

6. We learn in Alma that if a seed is good, it will begin to "swell within your breasts," which is how you will know the seed is good. In fact, we further learn in this verse that if the seed is good, it will enlarge your soul, enlighten your understanding, and be delicious to you (see Alma 32:28). Likewise, in a relationship, if the person you are dating is good, you will feel happiness and joy in your heart. Your soul will grow and expand as you become a better person. And you will feel happy and excited instead of fearful, worried, or scared. Furthermore, if the seed is good, it will sprout and grow, just as if a relationship is good, then it too, will sprout and grow, and eventually become a mighty tree. If you are with the right person, your relationship will progress and become stronger. You will become more unified, and your love will deepen for each other as time passes.

7. What are others saying about your relationship? If you want to ensure that your revelation to marry is not merely based on emotions, consider what those closest to you, who have your best interest at heart, are saying, or at least thinking. How do your parents and siblings feel about the person you are dating? What do your friends and roommates think about your potential marriage? What

are your Church leaders and other mentors saying about your relationship? Are they happy for you? Or do they have significant concerns?

There are many keys to help us understand the differences between emotions and spiritual promptings. The list I have provided is not comprehensive by any means. You can avoid being confused between emotions and spiritual promptings as you seek the Spirit, immerse yourself in the scriptures, and desire multiple witnesses. Strive to obtain the Spirit in your life daily by keeping your mind and body clean, avoiding sin and wickedness, feasting upon the words of Christ, and walking uprightly before God.[7] Stay on the straight and narrow path, hold on to the iron rod, and walk toward the tree, which, in this case, is marriage. Having the Holy Ghost with you will help you see things clearly, and you will feel the Lord's guidance and direction.

Thought Questions

1. Have you ever made a big decision in your life based on emotions?
2. Of the keys provided, which one do you believe will help you the most to distinguish between the voice of the Spirit and your own emotions? Why?

---

7. See Carlos Asay, "The Companionship of the Holy Ghost," *Ensign*, April 1988, 15–16.

10

Is it true that revelation often comes in small pieces instead of large doses?

Surprisingly, receiving answers to your prayers may not always come in one lump sum. Most often, revelation comes in increments—in small pieces along the way. The Lord rarely reveals His will to us in *one* large dose. Consider Nephi and his herculean task to build a ship. Did the Lord show him in one simple visit how to build a large, sea-worthy vessel? From the Book of Mormon, we learn that the Lord showed Nephi "from time to time" (1 Nephi 18:1) how he could construct a large ship.

Regarding the marriage decision, the Lord will also provide answers to you from "time to time." Elder Richard G. Scott declared, "When we seek inspiration to help make decisions, the Lord gives gentle promptings. These require us to think, to exercise faith, to work, to struggle at times, and to act. Seldom does the whole answer to a decisively important matter or complex problem come all at once. More often, it comes a piece at a time, without the end in sight."[1] Consider this formula as you contemplate the marriage decision. You may not learn from the Spirit all at once, but you will receive revelation step by step along the way.

---

1. Richard G. Scott, "Agency and Answers: Recognizing Revelation," *Ensign*, June 2014.

Incremental Revelation

Elder Scott additionally taught, "Seldom will you receive a complete response [to a prayer] all at once. It will come a piece at a time, in packets, so that you will grow in capacity. As each piece is followed in faith, you will be led to other portions until you have the whole answer. That pattern requires you to exercise faith in our Father's capacity to respond."[2] Even though most of us would like to know everything at once, the Lord will not quench our spiritual thirst with a firehose. Instead, the Lord often reveals His will to us gradually. My friend and colleague, Randal A. Wright, helped me to see the following pattern in the scriptures.

Consider that even Jesus Christ "received not the fulness at first, but continued from grace to grace, until he received a fulness" (D&C 93:13). When Joseph Smith asked where to build the Latter-day City of Zion, the Lord revealed it to him this way:

- **September 1830**: "It shall be on the borders by the Lamanites" (D&C 28:9).
- **June 1831:** "Ye shall assemble yourselves . . . to rejoice upon the land of Missouri, which is the land of your inheritance" (D&C 52:42).
- **July 1831:** "The place which is now called Independence is the center place, and a spot for the temple is lying westward" (D&C 57:3).

Why didn't the Lord just tell Joseph in September of 1830 that the city of Zion would be in Independence, Missouri? I am not exactly sure, but perhaps at that time, Joseph would not have known where Independence was. The Lord had to take Joseph, and the Saints, through a process before revealing the location of the city of Zion, when He knew they were ready to receive it.

---

2. Scott, *Ensign*, May 2007, 9.

DOES REVELATION OFTEN COME IN SMALL PIECES?

Many years ago, I took on a new job in the Dallas, Texas, area for the Church Educational System—now called Seminaries and Institutes. My assignment did not come with an instruction manual, and my specific area was unique compared to other areas in our region. Regularly, I prayed over my professional assignment as I sought for the Lord's will and direction. I did receive small revelations regarding the steps I should take in developing a new area and new program, but not as quickly as I had hoped. The Lord rolled out His plan for my assignment a piece at a time. I felt that every so often I was given another key revelation pertaining to my professional assignment. Eventually, the entire plan was in place, but that took several years. I often wondered why the Lord did not just tell me the entire plan my first week on the job—that would have made matters much easier. However, the Lord needed to know that He could trust me with each piece of information that He revealed to me. As I acted on those revelations, more divine direction came.

Elder David A. Bednar explained to college students that we tend to believe that "the Lord will give us a big answer quickly and all at one time. However, the pattern repeatedly described in the scriptures suggests we receive 'line upon line, precept upon precept,' or in other words, many small answers over a period of time. Recognizing and understanding this pattern is an important key to obtaining inspiration and help from the Holy Ghost." Elder Bednar went on to explain that most often, the Lord speaks to us through "ongoing, incremental, and unfolding pattern[s] of small answers."[3]

Elder Neal A. Maxwell quipped, "When the Lord gives us 'line upon line,' and 'precept upon precept' about Himself and His plans, many ignore these great gifts. Instead of lines, some

---

3. David A. Bednar, "Line Upon Line, Precept Upon Precept," BYU–Idaho Devotional Address, 11 September 2001; https://www2.byui.edu/Presentations/transcripts/devotionals/2001_09_11_bednar.htm

demand paragraphs or even pages. When God provides 'here a little, and there a little,' . . . some want a lot—now!"[4] When I was called to be a stake president, the Lord did not reveal to me or to my counselors, all at once, the plan and direction for our stake. The revelations certainly came incrementally. The initial revelation we received was to call and assemble a new high council. That became our first order of business. Next came the direction on how we should train bishops and other priesthood leaders in our stake. Following that came the inspiration on how we should approach ward conferences. If all of these events were revealed to us the first week on the job, I think we would have been so overwhelmed that we may have failed at everything. The Lord needed to know that He could trust us with the revelations He was giving us. Once that was established, revelation continued to come.

Be aware that the Lord will engage you in a similar process as you seek revelation on the marriage decision. He may not tell you all at once, but along the path, He will gradually reveal His will to you. Initially, you may feel that the person you are dating is a wonderful person. Soon thereafter, you may receive a revelation that informs you to continue the relationship. Perhaps later, you may receive a revelation that the individual you are dating is an outstanding person and that you should continue your relationship with them. Later, you may come to know that this individual would be an excellent wife/mother/husband/father. Even later, you may begin to feel strongly that you should marry them. There may be many other revelations that could fall between these larger ones. As you act on what the Lord reveals to you, He will give you more information, more direction, and more assurance. This pattern will not only pertain to your marriage decision, but you will feel it and experience it throughout your lives.

---

4. Neal A. Maxwell, *Neal A. Maxwell Quote Book*, 288.

DOES REVELATION OFTEN COME IN SMALL PIECES?

As you pray over the marriage decision, expect small pieces or "packets" of information to be revealed to you over time, rather than the entire "enchilada" all at once. Act on the answers that He gives you, and have the faith to move forward. If the Lord needs to stop you, He will. However, unless He does, full steam ahead.

Thought Questions

1. How has the Lord revealed things to you in the past "line upon line"?
2. Why do you feel the Lord reveals His will in this "incremental" fashion?

11

Can "instinct" be part of the revelatory process?

Sometimes in life, we tell individuals to "go with their gut." To go with your gut is to follow your instincts and to trust your feelings. What do your instincts tell you about the marriage decision? Does it feel right? Do you feel that deep down inside your soul, the decision is correct? What does your logic and reason tell you about the marriage decision? President Gordon B. Hinckley once explained that the marriage decision should be "guided by prayer as well as instinct."[1]

Twenty Questions

When I was contemplating asking Janie to marry me, my gut was ahead of my mind. I felt that the entire relationship made so much sense. I worked my way through a series of questions that helped me to make the proper decision. Here are some of those questions that I asked myself, and now, I ask you:

1. ***Are you attracted to him/her?*** This is not only physical. Also consider the individual's personality. In my case, I was very attracted to every aspect of Janie. I felt that she

---

1. Gordon B. Hinckley, "Life's Obligations," *Ensign*, February 1999, 2, 4.

was physically beautiful and had a wonderful personality. In fact, she was someone I admired and respected.

2. ***Are you in love with him/her?*** I know this sounds oversimplified, but you must ask yourself this question. Although love is hard to define, most people know it when they experience it. For me, I began to realize I was in love when I recognized that I never wanted to be apart from Janie and could not imagine life without her. I even wanted to be with her more than my friends and intramural teammates. I began to realize that I was in love and wanted to be with her for the rest of my life.

3. ***Are you best friends?*** Do you feel comfortable with each other? Can you be your unadorned, natural selves when in each other's presence? When couples become best friends, they realize that they can talk about anything and everything under the sun. One of the greatest things you can do in this life is marry your best friend.

4. ***Do your goals and dreams flow together?*** Are you heading in the same direction, and do you want the same things in life? Do your educational goals, family desires, and career dreams flow together? Do you feel that you are heading in the same direction? Can you see a wonderful future with this person?

5. ***Are you able to build each other up?*** Can you compliment and praise each other with ease? Can you inspire each other to be better? Happily married couples are comfortable giving each other praise and sincere compliments, and they certainly can validate each other. Do you want to be a better person because of your significant other? I remember just wanting to be the best person that I could be because I felt that Janie was so good.

Here are some other questions that should be considered:

6. *Have you been in each other's homes and observed the interactions between your future spouse and their parents and siblings?* Do you feel comfortable how your significant other treats their family members? Do you appear to have similar beliefs on how often you will see your families once you are married? What role will your families play in your future life together?
7. *How do you feel about your partner's friends?* Do you have similar views on the role friends could play in your future marriage? Are your partner's friends good people that will have a good influence on both of you? How does your partner feel about your friends?
8. *Have you been able to view each other during times of stress or crises?* How did your future partner handle those stresses? How do you handle stress? Do you feel comfortable with each other from what you have observed in this area?
9. *Do you and your partner work well as a team?* Have you worked together to improve something, like cleaning or building something? Have you worked together serving others, such as watching someone's children? Have you planned activities together, made meals, or worked on a project together? How did that go? Are you a good team?
10. *Have you taken a long trip together?* How did that go? Were you able to talk freely together? Did you feel any annoyance or irritation? Did you enjoy each other's company and feel you could talk for hours? Were you able to laugh together and understand each other? Did you feel more connected to each other by the time you arrived home? Did you learn that you have interests in the same areas?
11. *Have you been able to resolve conflicts?* How do you both deal with differences of opinion? Do you notice some flexibility in your future partner and their willingness to negotiate? Are you able to see their point of view? Are you empathetic toward them and the problem they were experiencing?

12. ***Do you appear to have similar views on managing money?*** Have you discussed finances with each other? If you were married, who would manage the money? Who would pay the bills? Who would do the shopping? How would you save or invest your money? What superfluous things would you like to purchase?
13. ***Do you appear to have similar views on when to have children and how to raise them?*** Have you discussed your parenting beliefs with each other? Do you know how many children you would like to have someday? How will you discipline, train, and teach your children? How will you build relationships with them? Do your beliefs on child rearing align?
14. ***Do you seem to have similar views of how you will practice your religion in the home?*** How will you keep the Sabbath Day holy? What role will scripture reading, singing, and prayer have in your household? What about how you serve in the Church? Are you willing to support each other in significant callings that require much time and energy? Do you feel united in this crucial area?
15. ***Do you seem to have similar views on how to have fun and recreate together?*** Do you seem to enjoy the same outdoor activities? What about indoor fun? Should you invite others when your families do fun activities? What if you do not enjoy the same kinds of recreational activities? Can you find common ground when it comes to recreation?
16. ***How do you both feel about the role education will play in your lives?*** What about future careers? Do either of you plan to go to graduate school? How will you emphasize education in the home? Who will help the children with their reading, writing, science, history, and math homework? How will you create a culture in your home of continually learning? Do you have similar beliefs when it comes to the role that education will have in your family?

17. ***How do you both feel about gender roles?*** Do you both want children? If you do have children, do you agree on who will stay home with the children and who will provide a living for the family? Are their traditional male roles that could be assumed by a future wife? Are their traditional female roles that could be embraced by a future husband? What will your gender roles look like in this relationship?

18. ***How do you both feel about physical health and wellness?*** Will exercise and eating healthy play a role in your future relationship? Would you like your children to participate in athletic events and sports? Will you and your spouse work out together or separately? How will you approach eating healthy? Who will watch the children when a spouse wants to exercise?

19. ***Are you both mentally and emotionally healthy?*** If not, can one partner help the other with their challenges and issues? Are you equipped to assist and nurture a future spouse who may be challenged with their mental health? Do you know how to nurture and strengthen each other during trials and challenges?

20. ***Do your political beliefs align?*** Do you see such beliefs as a source of contention or harmony in your future marriage? Can you talk about political issues in healthy ways? How much time will you spend listening to political talk radio and podcasts? Could you coexist if your political beliefs are very different?

Could the answers to these questions help you make a "common sense" decision on marriage? Obviously, you will want to receive a spiritual confirmation regarding the marriage decision. However, these "gut check" questions could also help your decision become clearer.

The Holy Ghost and Common Sense

President Dallin H. Oaks once taught that the Spirit will not give us revelations on trivial matters. He explained, "I once heard a young woman in testimony meeting praise the spirituality of her husband, indicating that he submitted every question to the Lord."[2] President Oaks then shared how this husband would join with his wife on trips to the grocery store. Apparently, he would not choose between different brands of canned vegetables without praying over the decision. Then, President Oaks concluded, "That strikes me as improper. I believe the Lord expects us to use the intelligence and experience he has given us to make these kinds of choices."[3] Yes, the Lord has given us fine, keen minds. He has provided us with experiences and instincts that will help us make the marriage decision. He trusts us to use our faculties, knowledge, and experiences to make wise choices.

Let me share with you how my instincts worked when I needed to make the marriage decision. Janie was beautiful, and I loved her personality. She was quiet but passionate about her beliefs, which also was attractive to me. I felt that our dreams and goals aligned well, and we both felt strongly about the family and the gospel of Jesus Christ. I could not stand to be away from her for prolonged periods of time, and I knew I wanted to spend the rest of my life with her. I also knew that if I married her, the gospel of Jesus Christ would be the center of our future family. Furthermore, I could not think of any reason why we should not marry each other. In practically every way, Janie was all that I ever wanted in a future wife. The thought of marrying her made me happy and excited about the future. My instincts told me that marrying her would be one of the greatest decisions of my

---

2. Dallin H. Oaks, "Revelation," *Brigham Young University 1981–1982 Speeches*, 29 September 1981, 7.
3. Ibid.

life, and it has been. Perhaps the biggest challenge of my life was convincing her to feel the same way.

Thought Questions

1. What do your instincts, experiences, and knowledge tell you about the person that you hope to marry?
2. What concerns do you have regarding the person you hope to marry? Can those issues be resolved?

12

What is the principle of stewardship in revelation?

Religious educator and administrator Gerald Lund shared the following experience. When he was teaching institute classes in Southern California years ago, a very common experience occurred quite frequently. A female student would approach him and explain that the young man she had been dating had received a revelation that they were to marry. Brother Lund then observed:

> The interesting thing to me was that often the girl felt intimidated by such a declaration, feeling that she needed to accept the "Lord's will" even though she found the prospect somewhat distasteful. [In some cases that was downright distasteful.] Some were even a little shocked when I boldly explained that unless they received an independent confirmation from the Lord, they should feel no pressure to accept the boy's request.[1]

Over the years, I have heard several experiences of women feeling obligated to marry men. Just because *he* had a revelation

---

1. Gerald N. Lund, "The Voice of the Lord," *Brigham Young University Speeches*, 2 December 1997.

they were to do so. One of those women asked a member of her stake presidency in her temple recommend interview just a few days prior to her wedding, "Is it all right to marry someone if you don't love them?" This young woman further explained to her priesthood leader that she was a new convert to the Church and did not seem to understand how to receive her own personal revelation. She said, "He and I both decided that because he held the priesthood, he had the authority to receive the correct answer to my prayer. And now I'm willing to marry him if that's what I'm supposed to do. But in all honesty, I must admit I don't love him."[2] Thankfully, this priesthood leader, Elder Bruce C. Hafen, was able to explain to the young man and the young women the principle of stewardship in revelation and instructed them to go back to the drawing board. If the revelation were true, Elder Hafen explained that it would be revealed to both of them. Ultimately, they terminated their relationship. Perhaps from this experience, we could create a general principle: *It is probably not a good idea to marry someone that you really do not like that much.*

Stewardship in Revelation: Men and Women

Year ago, shortly after retiring as President of Brigham Young University, Dallin H. Oaks, as a member of the Utah Supreme Court, returned to the campus to deliver a talk to the student body on the topic of revelation. He stated:

> Only the president of the Church receives revelation to guide the entire Church. Only the stake president receives revelation for the special guidance of the stake. The person who receives revelation for the ward is the bishop. For a family, it is the priesthood leadership of the family. Leaders receive revelation for their own stewardships. Individuals can receive revelation

---

2. Bruce C. Hafen, "Women, Feminism, and the Priesthood," audio cassette (Provo: Utah: BYU Media Services, 1985).

to guide their own lives. But when one person purports to receive revelation for another person outside his or her own stewardship—such as a Church member who claims to have revelation to guide the entire Church or a person who claims to have a revelation to guide another person over whom he or she has no presiding authority according to the order of the Church—you can be sure that such revelations are not from the Lord.[3]

Therefore, we can only receive revelations in the areas where we have responsibility, or stewardship.[4] As a husband, I can receive revelation for my marriage, and so can my wife—and she does. In fact, when it comes to our family, Janie and I both receive revelation for our family from time to time. As the president of my stake, I can receive revelation for my stake, but I cannot receive revelation for my students, my clients, or even my good friends. We can only receive revelation in areas where we have stewardship. President Oaks further explained:

> If a revelation is outside the limits of stewardship, you know it is not from the Lord, and you are not bound by it. I have heard of cases where a young man told a young woman she should marry him because he had received a revelation that she was to be his eternal companion. If this is a true revelation, it will be confirmed directly to the woman if she seeks to know. In the meantime, she is under no obligation to heed it. She should seek her own guidance and make up her own mind.[5]

As a professor at BYU, I have not met many female students lately who feel obligated to marry young men that have had a

---

3. Dallin H. Oaks, "Revelation," *Brigham Young University Speeches*, 29 September 1981.
4. See Mark D. Ogletree, *Preparing for Your Celestial Marriage* (American Fork, Utah: Covenant Communications, 2017), 184–85.
5. Oaks, 1981.

revelation about their future. It feels that our present generation of young people understand the principle of stewardship in revelation better than previous generations. Perhaps this can be attributed to excellent teaching in our homes, or the amount of young women who now serve missions and are well acquainted with the principles of revelation. Nevertheless, there is another area where I see the stewardship principle often misunderstood, and that is with well-meaning parents.

Stewardship in Revelation: Parents

Some parenting styles in recent years have proven to hinder a child's development and interfere with an adolescent's growth, maturity, and overall development. "Helicopter" parents hover over their children, paying close attention to their children's activities and schoolwork. Essentially, they are overly involved in their children's lives.[6] Similarly, a "snowplow" parent is one who seeks to remove all obstacles from their child's path so they do not experience "pain, failure, or discomfort."[7] Largely due to a generation of "helicopter" and "snowplow" parents, I often witness the problems that overinvolved parents create in their adult children's lives. Perhaps you have read some of the stories and experiences of such parents—negotiating the salaries for their thirty-year-old son or arguing with college professors over their twenty-three-year-old daughter's grades in a chemistry class at her university. Such over-parenting is not without some tragic consequences. Today, as a BYU professor, I see more parents getting in the way of their children's marriages than I have ever witnessed. In other words, the issue with "stewardship in

---

6. Amy Morin, "What is Helicopter Parenting," Verywell Family, https://www.verywellfamily.com/helicopter-parents-do-hey-help-or-hurt-kids-1095041; accessed 7 January 2022.
7. "What is Snowplow Parenting?" Grow by *Web*MD, accessed 7 January 2022; https://www.webmd.com/parenting/what-is-snowplow-parenting#1

revelation" is not a problem regarding a young man and young women. The present issue now regarding "stewardship in revelation" is between children and their parents.

I have had many students over the years come into my office and explain that they are very happy in their present relationship. They love their partner, and they are looking forward to marriage and a wonderful life together. However, one of their parents has "put their foot down," so to speak, and said that they do not feel good about the marriage. These parents often explain that they have prayed about the relationship and they cannot support it.

Too often, their reasoning is quite puzzling. Most parents are not opposing these marriages because they sense histories of violent crime, apostasy, mental illness, drug use, or Ponzi schemes. For instance, one mother said that she prayed about the relationship and did not feel good about it. Besides, the mother said, "We are supposed to travel Europe next summer, and if you get married, we won't be able to do that." A grandfather told his grandson, "Please do not marry her—she is not on our level." Another mother said to her daughter, "You can't marry him—you're too young." I asked this girl how old her mother was when she married. She said that her mother was twenty years old when she married. My student was twenty-two years old. I suggested to my student that she should call her mother and remind her of this basic math problem.

Another father said, "I cannot approve of this relationship, and the Spirit tells me it is wrong." The daughter pushed her father on this, asking him to be completely honest. Finally, the father said, "If you get married, I will miss you." I am happy that this father will miss his daughter—that is how it should be. I have seven daughters of my own, and of course, when they marry, I miss my day-to-day interactions with them. But they are not moving to Antarctica. I would never dream of keeping any of my daughters away from the chance to marry a worthy, mentally healthy, Melchizedek Priesthood holder in the temple.

I want them to make eternal covenants and begin to receive the same blessings that I have received by being married to a wonderful person. Once again, I understand the need for parents to intervene, and even protest, when their child is about to marry a thief, a serial killer, an abuser, or even someone who is potentially not going to be active in the Church. However, parents cannot get in the way of celestial marriages because it is going to ruin their family trip to Disneyland (Perhaps the mother was hoping she was going to sit next to her daughter on Pirates of the Caribbean—not her new son-in-law).

This leads us to an interesting concept. When do parents discontinue receiving revelation for their children? When they are twenty, thirty, or forty? I confess that I do not know the answer to this question. I would like to believe that parents should always be entitled to receive the Lord's guidance when it comes to their children, and even grandchildren. However, what should families do when the revelations they receive contradict each other?

Here are some things I do know. First, if a revelation is true, I believe both parents and their adult children should receive a witness of the truth. With our seven married children, Janie and I have always felt the peace that comes from the Holy Ghost, confirming the marriage to be right. Nevertheless, sometimes parents are not able to get on board because they see some red flags or some warnings. Perhaps there is some information parents may need before they can feel at peace. Moreover, there are legitimate occasions when parents see things that their children cannot see. Janie and I have had that experience as well, where we have had to help a child or two pull their head out of the clouds and face reality.

Recently, I met with a young female returned missionary in my counseling office. She was deeply in love with her boyfriend, and he was in love with her. One night, they were talking about their wedding plans and, even for fun, discussing the names of their future children. The next day, he broke up with her. What was the reason? His parents did not feel good about the marriage, saw some concerns, and simply instructed their son to pull the plug. So he did. There was no discussion with the young woman, no issues to resolve, just an "out-of-the-blue" break-up. It was devastating to her, and she has spent months trying to recover from that difficult experience. She felt rejected and less than good enough for this young man and his family. I am happy to report that today she is newly married to another young man and extremely happy.

If Janie's parents[8] received a "revelation" that we were not to marry, I would have done the following:

1. We would have had a meeting, face to face, where we could have discussed their fears and apprehensions. I would have done my best to answer their questions and resolve their concerns.
2. In that meeting, I would have made sure Janie and I demonstrated a wonderful, loving relationship. I would have wanted her parents to see how happy we were together.
3. I would have tried to handle the meeting with maturity and self-control. I would not let emotions take over, and no matter what happened, or how heated the discussion became, I would have tried to remain dignified and mature.
4. If we could not gain her parents' support, Janie and I would have gone back to the drawing board and had a discussion of what we felt we should do. If her parents' concerns were not legitimate, then we probably would have moved forward with faith and married in the temple

---

8. See Mark D. Ogletree, *Preparing for Your Celestial Marriage* (American Fork, Utah: Covenant Communications, 2017), 185–86.

without them. We would have prayed that her parents would come around.
5. If her parents' concerns were legitimate, then we would have gone to work on solving those problems. We would have called for another meeting a few months later to see, after some changes, if we had gained their support.
6. Ultimately, as adults ourselves, we would have to decide if we would let her parents stand in our way—especially since we felt so strongly about our decision, and since we felt the confirming influence of the Holy Ghost.

I hope that most of you will not have to experience what I have described in this chapter with your family. However, some of you will, and that is why I have written about it. No matter how difficult the issue, things can be worked out and resolved. The Lord will be with you in this process, and if the relationship is right, then the way will open up for the marriage to take place.

Thought Questions

1. Have you ever had experiences where you felt completely different from your parents on an issue? Can you look back and recognize if the Spirit was leading you? Were your parents following the Holy Ghost?
2. Have you received more than one witness that the course you are now pursuing is correct? How has the Spirit direct you on the path you are currently traversing?

13

What are some barriers to feeling the Holy Ghost?

Receiving revelation is certainly a learning process. I have learned that there can be many barriers to receiving revelation. Often, these barriers are self-imposed. We put these barriers in place, not our Father in Heaven. Some of these barriers are innocent, such as being fatigued, hungry, feeling overwhelmed, being stressed, or even anxious. We would do well to disconnect ourselves from the world, take a mental health day, get some rest, eat some good food, and then go about trying to reconnect with heaven. I have always believed that a long, hot evening shower and occasionally going to bed earlier than 10:00 p.m. can help us "reset" ourselves and cure a multitude of problems.

The Barrier of Busyness

One common barrier to revelation is busyness. Indeed, we can become so busy that we become immune to the gentle nudging of the Spirit. Busyness can rob of us of being able to detect revelation and being able to receive answers to our prayers. One of Satan's most potent tools in our modern era is distraction. If we become so busy with the minutiae of life, our ability to hear the Lord's voice will be drastically hindered. As young single adults, you may feel over-busy as you manage work, school, church, family, dating, and friends. There seems to never be enough time for "all of the above."

Years ago, Church leaders such as David O. McKay, Harold B. Lee, and most recently, Ezra Taft Benson, related the story of Bishop John Wells. Back in the early 1900s, Bishop Wells was a General Authority serving as the second counselor in the Presiding Bishopric of the Church. In 1915, John's son was killed in a railroad accident. Sister Wells could not be comforted and was in a state of deep despair after her son's funeral. However, not long after the funeral, Sister Wells was lying on her bed, grieving over the loss of her son. Her deceased son appeared to her and gave her great comfort. The son said to his mother, "Mother, do not mourn, do not cry. I am all right." Besides providing comfort, the son had another message to share. He told his mother that shortly after the accident, he realized that he was in another sphere. The son tried to reach his father and communicate with him, but he could not. President Ezra Taft Benson explained, "His father was so busy with the details of his office and work that he could not respond to the promptings. Therefore, the son had come to his mother."[1]

If a busy, righteous man who later became a General Authority could disconnect himself from receiving spiritual communication from the other side of the veil, then so could each of us. Many young single adults are busy with coursework, homework, papers, exams, work responsibilities, social activities, and even church assignments that they can easily become unaware of revelation directed toward them. President Henry B. Eyring explained, "Your problem and mine is not to get God to speak to us; few of us have reached the point where he has been

---

1. Ezra Taft Benson, "Seek the Spirit," *Ensign*, April 1988; see also David O. McKay, *Gospel Ideals*, Salt Lake City: *Improvement Era*, 1953, 525–26.

compelled to turn away from us. Our problem is to hear."[2] Each of us need to find ways to connect ourselves to heaven. How do we get into the proper condition to hear the Lord's voice?

Each of us needs to unplug from the distractions of the world and become reconnected to the scriptures and the words of our living prophets. We need to find ways to drink from the well of living water. We can surround ourselves with enlightening music and even quietness. We should take the time to ponder, think, and meditate on our lives and the Lord's will for our lives. Keep a notebook close by so that you can record the spiritual impressions you receive as you draw closer to the Spirit.

Contention, Anger, and Other Barriers

We know that contention is of the devil (see 3 Nephi 11:29). If we are contentious with others, especially with our significant other, then we may disconnect ourselves from the Spirit of the Lord. The display of anger is also a sure-fire way to drive the Spirit out of our lives. We should examine our lives for elements of anger and contention. A classic example of the barriers of anger and contention comes from the life of Joseph Smith. On one occasion, Joseph and Emma had a household disagreement. Later in the morning, when Joseph tried to translate the Book of Mormon, he still harbored ill feelings toward Emma. Consequently, he could not translate a single syllable from sacred record. Joseph understood why the heavens seemed to be silent; he knew had had separated himself from the Spirit. He went out into the orchard and prayed for forgiveness. One hour later, he went back into their home, feeling humble and repentant. He asked Emma to forgive him, which she did. "Then he went back upstairs where was able to translate without any difficulty."[3]

---

2. Henry B. Eyring, *To Draw Closer to God* (Salt Lake City: Deseret Book, 1997), 29.
3. "A Peaceful Heart," *Ensign*, September 1974; https://www.churchofjesuschrist.org/study/friend/1974/09/a-peaceful-heart?lang=eng

In our own lives, we too should repent of our anger, hostility, and contention toward others. As we purify our hearts, the Spirit of the Lord will return to our lives. As we repent, answers to our prayers will come more readily and more clearly. There are many other ways we can disconnect ourselves from the Spirit, including being unkind or mean-spirited. Being critical of others, complaining incessantly, gossiping, and speaking ill of others are common barriers to feeling the Spirit of the Lord.

Technology Barriers

When our children were teenagers, they would often lie on our couch or across the family room floor, consumed with their phones. They were either texting their friends, browsing the internet, or checking their social media feeds. Sometimes I would call our children by name, and they could not hear a word I was saying—and I have a loud voice. I would often ask them, "How will you ever feel the Spirit if you are on your phone every spare minute of your lives?" They never had a good answer. I feel that I warned my children on many occasions that their phone would prevent them from feeling the Spirit.

On one occasion, Elder Gerald Lund stated, "Noise is endemic in our society. We live in envelopes of outer noise. We play music in our homes and cars, we watch television while we study, we even have [smart phones] so we can carry this envelop of noise with us when we walk or jog. This is not a bad thing, but it may interfere at times with the quiet whisperings the Lord wants to give us."[4] Indeed, noise surrounds all of us. Sometimes we are victims when it comes to the environmental noise that is part of our culture. Unfortunately, all too often, we create the noise that encompasses us. It is a sad to see many members of

---

4. Gerald N. Lund, *The Voice of the Lord*, BYU Speeches, 2 December 1997; https://speeches.byu.edu/talks/gerald-n-lund/voice-lord/

the Church today using their smart phones during worship services and in other sacred settings—completely detaching themselves from the Lord's Spirit. I understand that many times, our church members are reading their scriptures or reviewing conference talks. However, I know firsthand that it can be tempting to check text messages, emails, and browse social media feeds while we sit in our sacred church services.

Elder M. Russell Ballard stated,

> Handheld devices, such as smartphones, are a blessing, but they can also distract us from hearing the "still, small voice." They need to be our servants, not our masters. . . . When smartphones begin to interfere with our relationships with friends and family—and even more importantly, with God—we need to make a change. For some of you, the adjustment will be slight; for others, it may be significant. I am also concerned that excessive text messaging, Facebooking, tweeting, and Instagramming are replacing talking—talking directly one to another and talking in prayer with our Heavenly Father and thinking about the things that matter most in life.[5]

Not only are these mediums keeping us from communicating with each other, but they may be one of the most significant barriers that disconnect us from communicating with God. President Russell M. Nelson stated: "We live in a world that is complex and increasingly contentious. The constant availability of social media and a twentyfour-hour news cycle bombard us with relentless messages. If we are to have any hope of sifting through the myriad of voices and the philosophies of men that attack truth, we must learn to receive revelation."[6] President

---

5. M. Russell Ballard, "Be Still, and Know That I Am God," Church Educational System Devotional for Young Adults, May 4, 2014, www.broadcasts.ChurchofJesusChrist.org
6. Russell M. Nelson, "Revelation for the Church, Revelation for Our Lives," *Ensign*, May 2018, 96.

Nelson then warned that "in coming days, it will not be possible to survive spiritually without the guiding, directing, comforting, and constant influence of the Holy Ghost."[7]

We all need balance in our lives, and too much of a good thing is probably "too much." Each of us need to create opportunities each day to connect with our Heavenly Father and feel His Spirit. If you find yourself doing the following things, you are probably addicted to your device:

- Checking your phone all day
- Attending to every alert or notification that pops up
- Experiencing phantom vibrations
- Looking at your phone each time you have a free minute or two

Learn to detox from your phone. Teach yourself to check your phone at certain times each day. You should have periods of time each day where your phone is not with you. Seek for the Spirit in your life. Removing your phone from your grasp may be the first step in reconnecting with heaven.

Sin as Perhaps the Greatest Barrier

Perhaps the most likely culprit from keeping us from receiving direction from the Spirit is sin. Indeed, transgression is a certain way to dull our spiritual senses and disconnect us from revelation. Doctrinally, we know that no unclean person can dwell with God (1 Nephi 10:20-21). Ironically, many LDS couples who are seeking answers to their prayers have separated themselves from the Spirit because of their transgressions. More specifically, if a couple is seeking a revelation on the marriage decision but is

---

7. Ibid., 96.

morally unclean, they will find it difficult to receive clear answers from their Father in Heaven.

Elder Richard G. Scott explained the relationship between revelation and transgression:

> A word of caution: Recognize that an individual who is violating commandments of the Lord will find it very difficult to discern a prompting of the Spirit from the powerful emotions that can be stimulated through transgression. I am confident that is one of the reasons that some marriages fail. Two individuals who have allowed themselves to violate the laws of chastity during courtship cannot expect to clearly perceive the answer to their prayer regarding marriage. Under such circumstances, seeking to discern the guidance of the Spirit is like trying to savor the delicate flavor of a raspberry while chewing on a red-hot jalapeño pepper.[8]

Did you catch what Elder Scott said? Some marriages fail because the couple assumed they were receiving guidance from the Lord, but they really were not. Instead, they confused powerful emotions with the Spirit of the Lord. Consequently, they decided to marry, but it was not the right thing. Tragically, their marriages ultimately ended in divorce. Elder Scott also made it clear that it will be difficult to receive a revelation if we are engaged in moral transgression.

In order to receive the revelation you desire, make sure you are in good standing before the Lord. If not, get your mind and your heart right. Repent of your sins and change your behaviors. In many cases, visiting with a loving and understanding bishop will help you get back on track and work through the repentance process. You will find more joy, happiness, and peace once you

---

8. Richard G. Scott, "Making the Right Choices," BYU Speeches, 13 January 2002; https://speeches.byu.edu/talks/richard-g-scott/making-right-choices/

have repented. Only then will you be able to feel clear and concise answers from the Spirit.

President Harold B. Lee taught us the need for personal worthiness when it comes to revelation:

> The Lord will guide us if we live right. The thing that all of us should strive for is to so live, keeping the commandments of the Lord, that He can answer our prayers. . . . If we will live worthy, then the Lord will guide us—by a personal appearance, or by His actual voice, or by His voice coming into our mind, or by impressions upon our heart and soul. . . . Yes, if we so live, the Lord will guide us for our salvation and for our benefit.[9]

Indeed, if we can keep our covenants and live the commandments to the best of our ability, repenting of our sins daily, the Lord will pour down His spirit upon us. Receiving guidance and direction from Him will bless your life and your future family. His guidance will certainly help you make the marriage decision, and every other decision in your life. Identify the barriers to revelation in your life and then take a course of action to become more in tune with the Spirit. Repentance allows us to make changes and adjustments in our lives. Such changes will allow us to be close to the Lord and the Holy Ghost.

Thought Questions

1. What are some of the barriers in your own life that can keep you from receiving revelation?
2. How can your purify your mind in heart in order to receive revelation more clearly?

---

9. Harold B. Lee, *Teachings of Harold B. Lee*, 417.

14

What is a stupor of thought?

Several years ago, one of my Brigham Young University students came to visit me in my office.[1] One of the first words out of my student's mouth was, "I think I am having a stupor thought." I explained to my student, just to calm his nerves, that I lived in a constant stupor of thought. He did not think my joke was particularly funny, so I moved deeper into our conversation. I asked my student to tell me more about his "stupor" and the surrounding circumstances. He explained to me that he was in the middle of making the marriage decision and that he felt that he was certainly experiencing a stupor of thought.

I asked him, "What does this stupor feel like?"

He said, "I just have some doubts and fears about marriage."

I assured him that everyone has such doubts, but then I explained, "I do not believe you are experiencing a stupor of thought." I then said, "A stupor is very different than what you have described."

He then asked the million-dollar question: "Then what is a stupor of thought?"

---

1. See Mark D. Ogletree, *Preparing for Your Celestial Marriage* (American Fork, Utah: Covenant Communications, 2017), 192–93.

I realized that I was actually in a "stupor" myself. The more I tried to explain to my student, I recognized that I did not fully comprehend the concept much more than he did.

I then said to my student, "I believe I need to study more about this principle. Let me go to work on it, and then come back in a day or two and I will have a better answer for you."

So, I went to work and learned all I could about a "stupor of thought." When my student came back a few days later, I was able to teach him 1) what a stupor of thought was and 2) assure him that he was not experiencing a stupor but just plain-old ordinary doubt and fear. He was able to overcome those fears and is happily married today. I will now share with the reader what I learned in my journey to understand a "stupor of thought."

A Stupor of Thought

Modern revelation is most helpful in understanding the concept of "a stupor of thought." In Doctrine and Covenants 9:8–9, we read:

> But, behold, I say unto you, that you must study it out in your mind; then you must ask me if it be right, and if it is right I will cause that your bosom shall burn within you; therefore, *you shall feel that it is right.*
>
> *But if it be not right you shall have no such feelings,* but you shall have a *stupor of thought that shall cause you to forget the thing which is wrong*; therefore, you cannot write that which is sacred save it be given you from me. (emphasis added)

From this verse, we understand a "stupor of thought" is associated with forgetfulness. This verse can be cross-referenced with Doctrine and Covenants 10:2, where we learn that "darkness" can also be related to a stupor of thought. One dictionary defines the word *stupor* as "a dazed state, a . . . lack of mental alertness."[2] Other synonyms for *stupor* include sluggish, apathy, numbness, and absence of the ability to feel, uninterested, dullness, lethargy, and inaction. Some dictionaries mention being "dulled" or "completely suspended."[3] Individuals have described a stupor as the inability to make sense out of something, feeling nothing at all, or just feeling "blah" or our contemporary "meh."

Nevertheless, going back to the scriptural definition in the Doctrine and Covenants, forgetfulness is one of the foundational concepts of a stupor of thought. One LDS author explained, "Possibly an analogy would be if we have experienced going to the refrigerator, opening the door, but forgetting what we went for. Furthermore, when a stupor of thought occurs, there is no desire to continue thinking on that subject. We lose interest."[4] There are two key concepts about the stupor of thought I would like to address. The first comes from Elder Richard G. Scott, who taught that a stupor of thought, for him, was "an unsettling, discomforting feeling."[5] The second is the feeling of "forgetfulness" that we have already highlighted, or a general lack of interest. I will discuss both of these concepts in more detail.

---

2. See *Encarta World English Dictionary*, s.v. "stupor," as cited in Lanae Valentine, *Brigham Young University Speeches*, "Discerning the Will of the Lord for Me," 29 June 2004; https://speeches.byu.edu/talks/lanae-valentine/discerning-will-lord/
3. Merriam-Webster Online Dictionary; https://www.merriam-webster.com/dictionary/stupor#synonyms
4. Erroll R. Fish, *Promptings of the Spirit* (Cogent Publishing: Mesa, Arizona, 1990), 95–96.
5. Richard G. Scott, "Using the Supernal Gift of Prayer," *Ensign*, May 2007; https://www.churchofjesuschrist.org/study/liahona/2007/05/using-the-supernal-gift-of-prayer.p26?lang=eng#p26

Feeling Unsettled

Elder Richard G. Scott stated that when he experienced a stupor of thought, he simply felt unsettled or discomforted. Perhaps many of us can relate to this feeling. Throughout our lives, we have made decisions or have even been in places where we have felt unsettled or uncomfortable. To me, this means that no matter what you do, you cannot feel calm or peaceful about the decision you have made. If you have made a bad decision, maybe you are having a hard time sleeping, or are even dreaming about your poor choice. Throughout the day, as you think about the decision, you feel worse instead of better. Regarding the decision you are trying to make, you cannot feel any peace or contentment.

Unfortunately, during the course of our married life, Janie and I have felt this unsettling feeling too often—especially when it comes to purchases. I felt it once when we purchased a car, and I have felt it at other times when we have made spontaneous purchases. Once in Mesa, Arizona, a door-to-door salesman convinced me that we needed a burglar alarm for our house. He played on my lowest instinct—fear. He convinced me that while I was away at work, a burglar was going to jump over my back fence, steal all of my possessions (which in those days were quite minimal), and then run off with my wife and children. I signed the dotted line, and then I immediately knew we had made huge mistake. For several nights in a row, I had a terrible feeling about this purchase. It wasn't that I was against burglar alarms—I think they are wonderful. It was that we had absolutely no money in those days, and really no way to pay the monthly payment. I had made a huge blunder, and I knew it. The best day of my life was when I paid that alarm system off.

In your life, you too will occasionally make poor decisions. Perhaps you can do better than I did. When you feel those feelings of darkness, or if you feel unsettled or uncomfortable, it is not of God, and you should move another direction. Sometimes individuals feel these feelings when making the marriage decision. If you can feel no peace and are completely unsettled, then back away for a few days and see if you can discover why. If there is an issue to resolve, determine if you can unravel it and solve it. Perhaps the decision is not right, or the timing is off. Do not ignore the uneasy feelings, but pay close attention to them. If you continue to feel disturbed, then you may need to end the relationship for a time, or permanently.

Over the years, I have had a significant number of couples in my counseling office who have told me that they had "unsettled" or "discomforting" feelings about their marriage decision, but they decided to marry in the temple anyway. In some cases, these individuals were in mediocre marriages and were making the best of it. Others were in rotten marriages and were contemplating divorce. Their terrible marriage had brought them back to the uncomfortable feelings they had about marrying in the first place.

Once again, doubt and fear about marriage are something most individuals will experience. Is the doubt and fear over something specific, or just getting married in general? Remember, the Lord deals with specifics, and if there is something specific that is disconcerting to you, pay close attention to it. Do not bury your head in the sand or ignore these signals the Lord may be sending to you. Sometimes, problems and issues that cause concern can be worked out. Other times, it will be necessary to end the relationship.

Forgetfulness

A few years ago, another student came to visit me in my office on campus. He, too, was having struggles with making the marriage decision. Although he was on the verge of engagement, he was not feeling excited about the prospects of his future marriage. When he would pray over the marriage decision, his mind would wander into other areas, and he would literally forget the reason he was praying in the first place. When he explained this phenomenon to me, I told him that I believed he was having a stupor of thought. I feel confident to state that if you are praying over one of the most important decisions in your life—marriage—and you literally forget what you are praying about during your prayer, then you probably should not be getting married. Unless you are in advanced stages of dementia at age twenty-three or have a severe case of ADHD, I believe you are experiencing a stupor of thought. Perhaps I can illustrate this concept with a personal experience.

Many years ago, I began to think deeply about where Janie and I should live permanently and raise our family. At the time, we lived in Mesa, Arizona, which was an amazing place. But for some reason, I had the feeling that we would not end up there for a long time. Looking back, in some ways, I wish we would have stayed their longer than we did, which was close to ten years.

Nevertheless, I had a student from Boise, Idaho, and the more he talked about Boise, the more enamored I became with the possibility of living there. This town seemed to have everything we wanted—a mild climate, yet it was in the mountains; lakes, golf, biking, snow skiing, water skiing, camping, and in those days, very affordable housing. I realized that we could live on an acre of land in a 4,000-square-foot home for almost half the price of what we were paying in Mesa.

After talking to my student several times and ordering every piece of material I could from the Chamber of Commerce (yes, no internet in those days), I studied out the possibility of moving to Boise. In a short time, I became obsessed about moving there and thought about it often for months and months. Eventually, that summer, Janie and took a trip to Boise. I had to feed my curiosity and whet my appetite. The town was everything I thought of, and even more. I loved our time there, and I believed it was certainly the place where we should live. I would just need to convince my employer to transfer us to Idaho!

However, there was one minor detail that I had not considered in all of our plans. I knew I wanted to obtain my PhD. At the time, I was finishing my master's program and was planning to obtain a doctorate degree. I contacted Boise State University and discovered that at that time (early 1990s), the university did not offer any PhD programs. My desire to receive my PhD was stronger than my dream to move to Boise. And that was it. As soon as I discovered that key piece of information, I never thought about moving to Boise, Idaho, ever again. It was as if I had completely forgotten about the idea of living there. The idea left me almost as quickly as it came. It was definitely a stupor of thought. Later, when I did finish my PhD, the idea of moving to Boise was still gone. By then, the "big boom" had taken place in that part of Idaho, and we could not have afforded housing there anyway. Instead, we moved back to our home state of Texas, raised most of our children there, and had a wonderful experience living among our friends and relatives. If anyone who reads this chapter is from Boise, please know that I still have fond feelings for that city. Maybe one day we will get there, but for now, I'll keep my nose to the grindstone here in Provo, and we'll see what the Lord has in store for us after we retire.

As you pray over the marriage decision, if you experience forgetfulness, feel apathetic, or simply seem to lack interest, you are most likely experiencing a stupor of thought. If there is a problem in the relationship that needs to be solved, then do what you can to make things better or improve the relationship. However, you may know deep in your heart that this potential marriage is not going to work. Your heart and soul are just not in it—and that is a sure way to know that you should not get married in the first place. Identify your feelings, express them to your partner, and then end the relationship. That would be the best thing for both of you. No one wants to be married to someone who doesn't seem to care that much about them or the relationship.

Thought Questions

1. Have you ever had any "bad" or "unsettling" feelings after a decision you have made? If so, what was your experience?
2. Have you ever experienced feelings of "forgetfulness" as you were praying over something important?

15

How can timing affect the marriage decision?

When it comes to making the marriage decision, timing is everything.[1] I believe that sometimes we may have chosen the right person, but the timing may not be right. For that reason, we may still feel frustrated and confused. Perhaps I can illustrate this principle with a personal experience.

I did not grow up as a member of The Church of Jesus Christ of Latter-day Saints. However, during my sophomore year of high school, I met a wonderful friend on our high school football team. My friend, whose name was Alan, was our quarterback, and I was a receiver. Alan and I spent many hours throwing passes to each other. Early in our association, I learned that my friend was a member of The Church of Jesus Christ of Latter-day Saints. Shortly after we met, Alan presented me with a Book of Mormon. He even talked to me about Moroni's promise and told me that as I read the Book of Mormon, I would feel this "burning of the bosom" and I would know that his Church was true. I can remember as a fifteen-year-old reading the Book of Mormon and feeling absolutely nothing. In those days, I was

---

1. See Mark D. Ogletree, *Preparing for Your Celestial Marriage* (American Fork, Utah: Covenant Communications, 2017), 187–88.

having trouble discerning the difference between the "burning of the bosom" and some heartburn I had from eating pepperoni pizza. Literally, I remember logically trying to figure out why I was not feeling anything significant. I gave the Book of Mormon a chance for a couple of weeks, but I never had a spiritual experience while reading it or praying about it. Obviously, I was not spiritually mature enough to receive an answer from the Spirit.

Nevertheless, I did not give up my interest in the Church. My relationship with Alan and some other Latter-day Saint friends continued to deepen, and I spent more time learning about the gospel for the next couple of years. Shortly after my high school graduation, I took a job as an oil field roustabout in West Texas. In that setting, at the age of eighteen, I began to read the Book of Mormon again. However, this experience was very different compared to my sophomore year in high school. As I read each page of the Book of Mormon, the Holy Ghost manifested to me in powerful, unmistakable ways that the book I was reading and the gospel it contained were true. I met with the missionaries and was taught the gospel of Jesus Christ. I was baptized a month later.

Why the difference between the ages of fifteen to eighteen? Why did the Holy Ghost *not* speak to me at age fifteen? Why *did* the Spirit testify to me at age eighteen? Looking back on this experience, I think I may understand the Lord's purposes. My parents were essentially anti-Mormon, and they were not happy with me investigating the Church. When I was fifteen, if I would have told my parents I wanted to join The Church of Jesus Christ of Latter-day Saints, they would not have allowed me. Secondly, even if they did permit me to join, living under their roof for the next several years would have been difficult to practice my newfound faith. I think we would have had several significant conflicts, and I often wonder if my fragile testimony would have survived during that impressionable time of my life.

President Dallin H. Oaks explained, "If we do the right thing at the wrong time, we can be frustrated and ineffective.

We can even be confused about whether we have made the right choice when what was wrong was not our choice but our timing."[2] This could explain why for me personally, the age of fifteen did not work, but the age of eighteen was the perfect time for me to join the Church. I was technically an adult and could make my own decisions. By joining the Church at age eighteen, I had one year to prepare for a mission, which I am happy to report that I did. One year later, at the age of nineteen, I was called to the Washington Seattle Mission. Had I joined the Church a couple of years later, I may have missed the incredible opportunities that my mission presented. Indeed, timing is everything. It made all of the difference during my conversion process, and it could become a crucial issue for you as you contemplate the marriage decision.

President Dallin H. Oaks further taught:

> Learning the importance of timing has been hard for me. I tend to think that whenever I have an idea it is time to proceed on it, and whenever there is a problem the sooner I confront it the better. When a task needs doing, I tend to think that it should be done now. I have had to learn that in most big decisions, what is most important is to do the right thing. Second, and only slightly behind the first, is to do the right thing at the right time. If we do the right thing at the wrong time, we can be frustrated and ineffective. We can even be confused about whether we have made the right choice when what was wrong was not our choice but our timing.[3]

I know many people who have become confused and frustrated because they feel they have not received an adequate or clear answer from the Holy Ghost. Perhaps a significant part of

---

2. Dallin H. Oaks, *Life's Lessons Learned* (Salt Lake City: Deseret Book, 2011), 120–21.
3. Ibid.

the process that they have not paid much attention to is timing—is this the right time for this event to occur?

Consider another example. Several years ago, I had a student in one of my classes come to visit me in my office. He was struggling with the marriage decision. He had baptized a girl while he was in high school, and they continued to date up until his mission. By the time he arrived home from the mission field, she had already planned their entire wedding—down to the napkin colors. After a brief time of post-mission courtship, he began to feel trapped and smothered.

I asked him in one of our conversations, "Do you feel more in love with this girl now than you did six months ago?"

He said, "No, I really don't."

I then asked if she had become his best friend.

He replied, "Not really."

I suggested that he needed to figure out his dilemma. I told him that one of his options would be to disconnect from the relationship for a time so that he could determine what he really wanted to do. He reported to me several weeks later that he had broken off the relationship. He seemed happier and lighter. I am sure he felt some freedom as well.

Ironically, a couple of years later, I was in a restaurant in St. George, Utah, with some members of my family. After ordering our food, I noticed my former student—the one who needed to get out of the relationship—sitting at the table with some of his friends. I approached him, and we spent some time catching up with each other. He then said, "Do you remember that girl that I broke up with a couple of years ago?" I told him that I did remember the situation. He said, "Well, we are now happily married." I was shocked, to say the least.

He and I talked about his marriage in more depth, and he confirmed to me that the timing a few years earlier was wrong. He related to me that after he broke up with her, he had some time to think about what he really wanted in life. He was given some space and eventually began dating other girls. Ultimately, he realized that he already had what he really wanted all along. He went back to his initial girlfriend to rekindle their love for each other. Thankfully, she was willing to take him back. Today, they have a wonderful marriage.

Elder Neal A. Maxwell once wrote, "The issue for us is trusting God enough to trust also His timing. If we can truly believe He has our welfare at heart, may we not let His plans unfold as He thinks best?"[4] Many of us do trust in our Father in Heaven, but we falsely assume that timing is an insignificant issue. Our modern prophets have taught us that timing can be a critical issue, and that we should consider the timing of every decision we make.

Elder Dallin H. Oaks added,

> Indeed, we cannot have true faith in the Lord without also having complete trust in the Lord's will and in the Lord's timing...Do not rely on planning every event of your life—even every important event. Stand ready to accept the Lord's planning and the agency of others in matters that inevitably affect you....Anchor your life to eternal principles, and act upon those principles whatever the circumstances and whatever the actions of others. Then you can await the Lord's timing and be sure of the outcome in eternity.[5]

If you feel you are with the right person, but for some reason, things do not seem to be falling into place, consider the issue of timing. My daughter McKenzie dated a young returned missionary named Jared for several months. For different reasons, they broke the relationship off and moved on with their lives. Both decided that it was time to date other people. However, about a year later, our daughter posted something on social media

---

4. Neal A. Maxwell, *Even As I Am* (Salt Lake City: Deseret Book, 1982), 93.
5. Dallin H. Oaks, "Timing," Brigham Young University Devotional, 29 January 2002; https://speeches.byu.edu/talks/dallin-h-oaks/timing/

and Jared responded to her post. Within a few weeks, they were dating again seriously. That was in the early fall. By the following May, they were married in the temple. Today, they have three wonderful children. I believe that timing can be everything! If you are in a relationship presently, and for some reason, it may not be working out, do not discount the principle of timing.

Thought Questions

1. Have you ever had experiences in your life where you recognized that it wasn't the right time?
2. What experiences with right or wrong timing have you encountered?

16

How can I receive personal revelation?

Too many members of the Church view revelation as an event, rather than a process. Some suppose that to make the marriage decision, they need to hike up on top of a mountain, sequester themselves in the temple, or literally find their own sacred grove in order to receive the powerful confirmation they desire. Other individuals like to make receiving a revelation an all-day event. In fact, they seem to be looking for a Pentecostal experience. I am not saying that those who take these dramatic steps cannot get the revelation they are seeking—I am sure they can. However, what I am suggesting is that for most of us, revelation is a process rather than a one-time event. In fact, manifestations from the Holy Ghost do not usually come in the form of one large, mammoth revelation but many small ones that accrue over time.

As a new stake presidency, my counselors and I were faced with the task of selecting a new bishop for a particular ward. As a presidency, we did not trudge up to the top of Y-Mountain to receive our revelation, nor did we go to the temple. Unfortunately, temples were closed during this time. Instead, it was a slow and tedious process. First, I began to have some ideas of who the new bishop should be during the month of November. In December, I had lunch with the soon-to-be-released bishop and received some significant input from him. We both seemed to feel strongly about "Brother A," but I did not act yet. I wanted my counselors to be part of the process. Through the month of January, my counselors and I discussed the matter in depth and prayed together as a presidency. In February, we took a list of ten potential names into a presidency meeting and narrowed them down to four. By mid-February, we narrowed our list from four to one—"Brother A," the man I had felt good about since November. We prayed as a presidency over this issue several times and felt tremendous peace and a confirmation that he was the right man. One evening, in the high council room, we presented this man's name to the Lord, and we all felt a powerful witness that he was to be the new bishop. We submitted his name to the First Presidency, and by March, he was called to be the bishop of his ward. A process that began in November took several months of studying the issues and personalities, praying and fasting, and deliberating together as a presidency. There were many revelations and confirmations given along the way to help us understand that we had called the man the Lord had already chosen and prepared. Again, revelation is not usually a one-time event—it is a process.

As you approach the marriage decision, be willing to engage in such a process. This is not a one-time prayer but many prayers over a period of several months. Until the Lord stops you, continue to move toward temple marriage. It is likely you will offer many prayers over months and weeks as you seek the Lord's will. And He will reveal His will to you.

How to Receive Revelation

How can you prepare yourself to receive revelation? Obviously, you will want to be worthy so the Lord can reveal His will to you. Elder Boyd K. Packer expressed that if you "desire the inspiration of the Lord in this crucial decision, [you] must live the standards of the Church."[1] As I have mentioned before in this book, you certainly want to surround yourselves in a spiritual environment, with wholesome entertainment, uplifting music, and perhaps some order to your room or home. Strive for moral cleanliness and purity so the Lord can speak to you with clarity. Furthermore, you should also strive to create a spiritual climate around you, free from the distractions of the world and the temptations of the evil one. In addition, when you pray, you will want to listen—really listen—to what our Father in Heaven needs to reveal to you. Pay close attention to the thoughts and feelings you experience. Furthermore, do not rule out your "gut" feelings and instincts.

Many years ago, Elder Bruce R. McConkie shared a simple formula to receive revelation:

1. Search the scriptures.
2. Keep the commandments.
3. Ask in faith.

He then stated, "Any person who will do this will get his heart so in tune with the Infinite that there will come into his being . . . the eternal realities of religion. And as [he or she] progresses and advances and comes nearer to God, there will be a day when [he or she] will entertain angels, when [he or she] will see visions, and the final end is to view the face of God."[2] Elder McConkie's formula is something that we should all experiment upon and put to the test. I know the Lord will bless us, inform us, and reveal his will to us.

The right to receive personal revelation is open to every worthy member of the Church. In fact, anyone can receive

---

1. Boyd K. Packer, *Eternal Love* (Salt Lake City: Deseret Book, 1973), 11.
2. Bruce R. McConkie, "How to Get Personal Revelation," *Ensign,* June 1980; https://www.churchofjesuschrist.org/study/new-era/1980/06/how-to-get-personal-revelation?lang=eng

communication from God if they are willing to put forth the effort required. President Spencer W. Kimball promised, "God reveals himself to [people] who are prepared for such manifestations."[3] Therefore, let us prepare to receive a revelation, and get into the spiritual condition required to receive such a manifestation. President Brigham Young taught that when it comes to receiving personal revelation, many of us "live far beneath our privileges."[4] Most of us could do better at receiving personal revelation for our lives. This is a quest we should continually strive for.

Moreover, as members of The Church of Jesus Christ of Latter-day Saints, most of us have been baptized and confirmed. We have been given the gift of the Holy Ghost—our constant companion. If we live right, then we will always have His Spirit to be with us, especially as we make such significant decisions, such as marriage. You have the right to receive revelation for your own personal life, just as the prophet has the privilege of receiving revelation for the Church. Trust in the Lord. He will lead you along the safe path, and He will reveal His will to you.

The Revelatory Process

Step 1: Study out your decision.

The first step of the revelatory is to study out your decision. The Lord told Oliver Cowdery, "You must study it out in your mind" (Doctrine and Covenants 9:8). Therefore, gather information as you pray for direction. Search the scriptures, and talk to friends and associates. Seek the counsel of your bishop and others. Discuss the issue with parents, mentors, and others that you admire and trust. Tell them what you are planning to do or what you feel you are being led to do. Consider the long-term

---

3. Spencer W. Kimball, *Conference Report*, April 1964, 97.
4. Brigham Young, *Discourses of Brigham Young*, 32.

impact of your decision. How are the people you love the most responding to your decision?

Just a warning. Sometimes, not all counsel is good counsel. In fact, when receiving guidance from others, we must always weigh the good with the bad and make our own conclusions. For example, when Janie and I were approaching the marriage decision, I had a very meddling grandmother tell me I was making a huge mistake. She was not a member of our church, and she did not understand our view of temple marriage. Her counsel was useless for us.

Another member of Janie's side of the family also suggested we were too young to marry. Oh well, good thing we did not care much about what these people had to say. We felt that marrying was the right thing to do, and we were not going to let some distant cousin or an opinionated grandma stand in our way. Sometimes people do not have your best interests at heart; others are not aware of the spiritual experiences you have had with the decision you are making. Often, people do not know enough about your life to give you such significant advice. Be selective in whom you choose to give you advice.

Step 2: Make a decision.

Although I have already emphasized this concept throughout this book, it is worth repeating. The Lord has given us a fine mind, His spirit, and wonderful people around us. Using the resources the Lord has placed before you, make a decision. Understand the balance between agency and inspiration. We make our own choices, and then we present our decision to the Lord to receive His approval.

What is best for you? What is best for your partner? What do they want? What do you want? Gather the information, examine it, and make your choice. Ultimately, it is up to you to decide whom you will marry for all eternity.

Step 3: Present your decision to the Lord.

Through the medium of prayer, present your decision to the Lord. Tell Him how you feel about marrying your significant other. Ask your Father in Heaven how He feels about your decision. Is it right? Do you have His blessing? Would this marriage work, and would it be a happy one? Listen for His answer. Remember, this is not a one-time experience but hopefully a prayer you have offered many times. Our Father in Heaven wants you to be happy, and He will bless you with an answer.

Step 4: Receive a confirmation.

Confirmations may come immediately after your prayer (sometimes even during), hours later, days later, or even weeks later. Remember, we cannot dictate to our Father in Heaven when He will speak to us. Only He controls when these revelations come. Furthermore, remember that confirmations can come in many forms or fashions. Perhaps you will receive a warm, peaceful feeling. Maybe you will be overwhelmed with joy or happiness. For some, thoughts will enter their minds, such as "Yes, this is right," "Of course," or "Go forward with faith." Other will experience tears of joy and gladness, while some may feel a great sense of peace. Not all confirmations will come while you are on your knees in prayer. Sometimes they occur in the most unexpected places. In fact, confirmations could come in the dreams of the night, while you are walking to school or driving to work, while you are engaged in exercise or physical activity, while on a hike, when in the temple, or reading scriptures, or my favorite—while listening to general conference. I think many of the confirmations I have received in my life have come while I was laboring—working in yard, washing the car, or painting a bedroom. Be prepared to receive these promptings. Write the answer to your prayers in your journal, or record it somewhere. You will always want to look back to this spiritual experience.

Seek for multiple witnesses—not just one. We learn in the scriptures that "in the mouth of two or three witnesses shall every word be established" (1 Corinthians 13:1; Doctrine and Covenants 6:28). Confirmations can come multiple times, from multiple sources, and from multiple directions. Yes, confirmations can come more than one time, and that is something you should desire. Confirmations can come from multiple sources—from the Lord, experiences you have, something you heard in general conference, a scripture, a conversation with a friend, and even a line in a movie. Confirmations can come from multiple directions—meaning, from the Spirit, friends, family, music, and other media. Be open to receiving revelation from many different places and directions.

Step 5: Make sure the confirmation comes to both parties.

Obviously, your partner needs to experience this same revelatory process and receive their own answer. Do whatever you can to help them obtain a confirmation. This could mean answering questions, discussing the revelatory process, or helping resolve concerns.

In some cases, it could mean getting out of their way and giving them space. When Janie and I were trying to find out if we should marry, I felt I received my answer clearly and quickly, but she was struggling to obtain her own answer. Instead of hounding her, trying to convince her, or manipulating her, I deeply desired for her to receive her own revelation. I encouraged her to take all the time she needed. I did not want to sway her decision in either direction. I backed out of our relationship for a short period to remove all interference. I was prepared to keep my distance for a week or two, but in a matter of a few days, Janie received her answer. Giving her some space made all the difference.

Step 6: Move forward with faith.

Once you have received a confirmation, move forward with faith. Do not let Satan enter your mind or heart and "hijack" your spiritual experience. Furthermore, do not make the mistake of believing that once you receive a confirmation, everything in your relationship will be wonderful and exhilarating. You will still have challenges to work through and obstacles to overcome. When you receive a confirmation, Heavenly Father is telling you that the relationship is right and that you have His approval to move forward. However, the confirmation is not an award for awesome behavior or a predictor of a perfect relationship. You may find that you still have many things to work through, problems to solve, and adjustments to make. Trust in the Lord and move forward with faith. He wants you to be together, and He certainly wants you to be happy. He will help you along the way as you walk on the strait and narrow path. I have no doubt that the future looks bright and the Lord has great blessings in store for you.

Thought Questions

1. What experiences have you had that have helped you understand that revelation is a process?
2. How does the Lord most often speak to you?

17

Could Heavenly Father give us confusing answers?

Many problems in life stem from not understanding the nature of God, or better yet, His divine nature. For example, many people feel that their Heavenly Father is still punishing them for decisions they made a long time ago or for sins they committed when they were teenagers. Some adults in the Church still believe that they cannot be forgiven of sins they committed when they were in high school or college. Some feel that since they are not perfect, their Father in Heaven looks down on them. Still, others feel that they will never measure up and that they have no chance of making it to the celestial kingdom.

Several years ago, I met with a sixteen-year-old young man in my counseling office. He had broken the law of chastity several times and was really struggling with a pornography addiction. As we discussed his challenges, he broke down into tears and said, "I know that God hates me." I tried to provide comfort to this young man. When he composed himself, I attempted to straighten out his faulty thinking. I told him that I did not think he knew God that well. I testified to him that our Father in Heaven is the kindest, most merciful being he could ever meet. I explained that Heavenly Father is full of charity, patience, love, and acceptance. Furthermore, our Father in Heaven, I explained, is the most hopeful, optimistic, and faith-filled being you would ever meet. He believes in each one of us, and He has faith that we will accomplish what He has sent us here to do. Our God is kind, loving, and extremely forgiving. The young man whom I was working with felt comforted and began to feel for the first time that his Heavenly Father was on his side and pulling for him.

Over the years, as a bishop and as a therapist, I have learned that too many Latter-day Saints do not understand the true nature of the God we worship. Some see Him as a mean ogre, either who wants to punish us, or who does not care much for us. Others see Him as full of vengeance, judgment, or harshness. Still, others believe He is out in the universe somewhere but largely inattentive to our lives. I have had to ask myself, "Do members of the Church even know their Father in Heaven?" Sometimes, I do not think we do.

Consider what prophets and apostles have said about our Father in Heaven over the years. President George Q. Cannon declared, "No matter how serious the trial, how deep the distress, how great the affliction, [God] will never desert us. He never has, and He never will. He cannot do it. It is not His character [to do so].[1] What kind of God would never desert us? The kind of God who loves us more than we can comprehend.

Similarly, Elder Jeffrey R. Holland testified, "Just because God is God, just because Christ is Christ, they cannot do other than care for us and bless us and help us if we will but come unto them, approaching their throne of grace in meekness and lowliness of heart. They can't help but bless us. They have to. It is their nature."[2] What kind of God could only bless us—never curse us—but bless us? The kind of God who loves us unconditionally

---

1. George Q. Cannon, "Freedom of the Saints," in *Collected Discourses*, comp. Brian H. Stuy, 5 vols. (1987–92), 2:185.
2. Jeffrey R. Holland, "Come Unto Me," *Ensign*, April 1998, 19.

and wants to bless us. In the *Lectures on Faith*, Joseph Smith used these words to describe our Heavenly Father:

- Merciful
- Gracious
- Slow to anger
- No respecter of persons
- He is love
- Long suffering
- Full of goodness
- Forgiving[3]

Do these descriptions describe a God who does not really care about us, or who does not really like us? What about a God who simply wants to punish us like an angry army drill sergeant? I believe that if we could see our Father in Heaven, we would experience the most kind, loving, forgiving, hopeful, happy, and most optimistic being one could ever encounter. In fact, what we would feel most of all would be love. The love we would experience in His presence would probably bring us to our knees. Is this the God that you know?

With these doctrines laid as a foundation, let me share a common scenario I see often among my Brigham Young University students. In describing this scenario, I will use fictitious names. Jared and Kimberly are a wonderful couple who are madly in love with each other. They have been dating each other for several months, and, of course, they met in their family home evening group. They are both attracted to each other physically, and they communicate very well. In fact, they can talk about anything and everything with ease. They both love the gospel and frequently share stories and experiences from their missions with each other. They laugh a

---

3. Joseph Smith, *Lectures on Faith* (Salt Lake City: Deseret Book, 185), 3:12–20.

lot, and they enjoy doing fun things together. Their goals and dreams flow together very well, and many of their friends are eagerly anticipating their engagement soon. Then, one day, Jared was praying over the relationship and felt that Heavenly Father no longer wanted them together. The next day, he told Kimberly that they needed to break up. When she asked him why, he explained, "I prayed to determine if we should marry, and God told me *no*. In fact, He said that you, Kimberly, are not the one."

Let's dissect this experience—one that I have seen repeatedly as a Brigham Young University professor. First, if God really does tell you that the person you are dating is the wrong one, do not tell them that! That is just not nice! Come up with another excuse. Telling another person that God said they are not worthy to marry you is an extremely harsh and egotistical statement.

Second, would our loving Heavenly Father really tell an otherwise happy couple that they are not to marry? Would our Father in Heaven orchestrate events so that a couple could miraculously find each other, have a wonderful time together, have their goals and dreams flow together, have them be crazy about each other, have them fall in love with each other, and then say, "Just kidding. I tricked you guys, didn't I? That was a good one!" That is not the God that I know, and it is certainly not the God that I worship. Our Father in Heaven does not play games when it comes to eternal marriage. Our Father in Heaven is not out to trick us or play practical jokes on us. Elder Jeffrey R. Holland once said about our Father in Heaven, "He is not some sort of divine referee trying to tag us off third base."[4] A God that plays tricks on His children would be cause for great concern.

---

4. Jeffrey R. Holland, "Look to God and Live," *Ensign*, November 1993; https://www.churchofjesuschrist.org/study/general-conference/1993/10/

Likewise, a former apostle, Elder Richard L. Evans, once stated, "Our Father in heaven is not an umpire who is trying to count us out. He is not a competitor who is trying to outsmart us. He is not a prosecutor who is trying to convict us. He is a loving Father who wants our happiness and eternal progress, and who will help us all he can if we will but give him in our lives an opportunity to do so."[5]

Our Heavenly Father wants you to be happy, and if you are happy with a boyfriend or girlfriend, and the relationship is healthy and wholesome, He is not going to tell you to terminate the relationship. A significant part of the confirmation is that you are happy, you are in love, you are attracted to each other, and you want to spend every waking hour together.

On the other hand, if our Father in Heaven is aware of a significant personality flaw, a serious addiction, or some kind of psychotic behavior and He needs to warn individuals to terminate a relationship, He will do it. However, this tendency is probably more the exception, rather than the rule. To most couples who are happy, deeply in love, and are so good for each other, a loving God is not going to pull the rug out from such a couple and say, "I was just testing you—now go and find someone else." God does not work that way. He is a God that deeply desires for us to be happy, joyful, and successful.

Learn to walk by faith and see your relationship through the lens of faith. Believe that our Father in Heaven is in the details of your relationship. Have faith that He is the reason you met in such a miraculous way. Believe that He is the reason you cannot stand to be apart from each other. Come to understand that God is the reason your heart skips a beat when you see each other, and that He is the cause of your dreams, goals, and aspirations all flowing so well together. Heavenly Father is in the details of

---

look-to-god-and-live?lang=eng
5. Richard L. Evans, *Conference Report*, October 1956, 99–101.

your life. Believe in that, and believe that God wants you to feel happy, safe, and secure.

Thought Questions

1. Are you aware of completely happy couples who have broken up because "God told them to"?
2. How do you view our Father in Heaven? If you were to visualize Him walking into your home, what would He be like in appearance, in form, in personality, and in demeanor?

18

What roles can doubt, worry, and fear play in the marriage decision?

Often, couples will buy into the mistaken belief that once they have navigated their way through the marriage decision and have felt the inspiration and guidance of the Spirit, that everything will be perfectly calm and peaceful on their walk toward temple marriage. Then, when trials, worries, doubts, fears, and other obstacles fall into their path, one of their first thoughts is that perhaps they have made the wrong decision. Couples begin to think, "Maybe we should not get married after all!" Please remember that Satan does not want you to be happy. His entire mission is to ruin your life. Satan will oppose anything that is good for us or that will bring us closer to God. Satan does not want you to be happy, and he certainly does not want you to marry in the holy temple. He will do all in his power to keep you from reaching our Father in Heaven's holy house and being married for all eternity.

Doubts, Fears, and Worries

I am not aware of any engaged couples who have not had several doubts and worries about their future marriage. Often, during the engagement, some couples begin to question the spiritual answers they have received. Some may ask, "Was that answer from God, or was it just me?" Others forget all of the positive reasons for marriage and begin to focus on too many negatives and potential problems. Some individuals, of course, may begin question if they are marrying the right person. Some may fear that the possibility of having a good marriage is actually quite unlikely. Still, others are fearful that they will not be able to make things work out financially as they begin crunching the numbers. However, to solely focus on every bad thing that could potentially happen is not healthy, or helpful. Besides, most of the things that we worry about do not happen anyway. Only Satan would have you focus on everything negative and ignore the many positive reasons for your future marriage.

Some of us just need to relax. I use the word "us" because I also had some doubts and fears about my own marriage one week prior to our wedding. Deep into our engagement, I came to understand that Janie had always hoped and dreamed of serving a mission. I began to feel that I would be the one standing in the way of her being able to do that. Keeping my future wife from serving a mission was a terrible prospect, and I began to get a brain cramp about our relationship. She assured me that she would rather marry me than go on a mission. Since Janie was nineteen years old at the time, in those days she would have had to wait two more years to fill out her missionary papers and serve an eighteen-month mission. We would resume our relationship after she returned. The prospect of waiting almost four more years to marry seemed impractical—and it still does. We concluded that there was no way the Lord put us in each other's path when He did, only to wait for such a long time to marry. Janie also let me know that there was a rule written somewhere that you cannot bail out on a marriage one week before the wedding, and I believed her! Besides, she also told me that if I pulled the plug now, her dad would kick my tail! She reminded me on how much money her parents had already spent on the wedding, and if I pulled the "eject lever" now, it would not be a pleasant situation for many people involved. I came to understand that my own anxiety had gotten the best of me, and besides, who wants to be beaten up by a middle-aged angry dad?

Anxiety is real, and many individuals experience anxious symptoms during the engagement. Their self-talk is full of doubt, fear, and concern. Sometimes just talking about marriage can "creep out" some people. Some may even experience some of the physical symptoms of anxiety, which includes not sleeping well, being tired or fatigued, having difficulty concentrating, having headaches, having a racing heart, sweating, and even having digestive issues. Yes, anxiety can wreak havoc on your body.

Dr. Debra Theobald McClendon, a psychologist in Utah Valley, offered the following suggestions to help individuals discern between anxiety and feelings from the Spirit. First, she said you must cultivate awareness and come to understand that your anxiety is talking. Label these thoughts and feelings as "anxious" so that you can begin to deal with them. Second, choose behaviors to help your body relax, such as deep breathing, going for a walk, listening to calming music, exercising, and other relaxing activities. Third, Dr. McClendon stated,

> Once you feel calmer, another helpful step is to evaluate your thoughts. What are you telling yourself? Are your thoughts comforting, faithful, or reality-based? Or are they negative, condemning, and full of untruths or partial truths that are only escalating your anxiety? If you realize that your thoughts are distorted and making things worse for you, then clean them up! One way to do this is to write every piece of evidence you can think of to prove that the thought causing you distress is *not* 100-percent true. As you seek this evidence, in time the thought that is escalating your anxiety will lose power.[1]

---

1. Debra Theobald McClendon, "Discerning Your Feelings: Anxiety or the Spirit?" *Ensign,* February 2021.

Consider the following key from George Q. Cannon. He explained, "Whenever darkness fills our minds, we may know that we are not possessed with the Spirit of God. . . . When we are filled with the Spirit of God we are filled with joy, with peace, and with happiness, no matter what our circumstances may be."[2] Most often, darkness and confusion come from Satan, not from our Father in Heaven. When we feel love, light, and peace, rest assured your Heavenly Father is influencing you. Furthermore, our Father in Heaven does not speak in anxious, worrisome tones. Worry comes from Satan, not from God. God is all about love, and Satan is all about fear. If Heavenly Father needed to warn you about a disastrous decision or event, He would not do it through anxious self-talk. He would deliver the message through the Holy Ghost, in calm, peaceful tones. God is not anxious. For example, if your house was burning down and you were away from home, Heavenly Father would tell you through the quiet, calm voice of the Spirit—not by yelling or screaming at you.

Here is another key: Ask yourself, "Are my fears and doubts over generalities or specifics?" I once heard Michael Wilcox teach that God works in specifics, not generalities. So, if you have a very specific concern, pay close attention. Perhaps the concern is something that could be addressed, worked on, and improved. However, if you concern is more general, such as, "I'm just worried about getting married," then that message is probably not coming from God.

After receiving a revelation to marry, no one is going to skip down the road, directly to the temple, without any opposition. We will always have trials of our faith—in every decision we make. However, one major purpose of being on this earth is to learn to exercise faith. Anytime we need to exercise faith, there will be opposition—Satan will make sure of that.

---

2. In Brian H. Stuy, comp. *Collected Discourses Delivered by President Wilford Woodruff, His Two Counselors, the Twelve Apostles, and Others*, 5 Vols., 4:137.

Elder Gene R. Cook explained, "Tribulation is a refiner of faith. The Lord said, 'For after much tribulation come the blessings' (D&C 58:4). The Lord will never tempt a person, but He will try him. Tribulations and problems are what this earthly school is made of. Life is all upstream—all uphill. . . . The challenges and difficulties that many of us resist are the very elements that refine us and make us godly."[3] Of course, we will have tribulations and trials of our faith—especially regarding the marriage decision. Just expect that. However, such challenges do not mean your decision is incorrect. In fact, when such trials come, we should buckle up and recognize that if Satan is trying this hard to oppose our decision, then it has to be from God. Otherwise, why all of the opposition? We need to trust in God's revelation to us. Strive to believe wholeheartedly that our Father in Heaven wants you to marry one of his righteous children in His holy house. You will always be blessed for keeping His commandments.

President Thomas S. Monson once provided this counsel to those who are fearful to marry:

> I realize there are many reasons why you may be hesitating to take that step of getting married. If you are concerned about providing financially for a wife and family, may I assure you that there is no shame in a couple having to scrimp and save. It is generally during these challenging times that you will grow closer together as you learn to sacrifice and to make difficult decisions. Perhaps you are afraid of making the wrong choice. To this I say that you need to exercise faith. Find someone with whom you can be compatible. Realize that you will not be able to anticipate every challenge which may arise, but be assured that almost anything can be worked out if you are resourceful and if you are committed to making your marriage work.[4]

---

3. Gene R. Cook, *Faith* (Salt Lake City: Deseret Book, 1983), 101–102.
4. Thomas S. Monson, "Priesthood Power," *Ensign*, May 2011, 67.

As President Monson indicated, place your challenges and burdens upon the Lord, and find ways to move forward with faith. Every relationship we have in this life will often pose some kind of challenge. Nevertheless, move forward with faith, and the Lord will continue to bless you. Elder Jeffrey R. Holland once warned the students at Brigham Young University that satanic opposition often comes "*after* enlightened decisions have been made, *after* moments of revelation and conviction have given us a peace and an assurance we thought we would never lose."[5] Elder Holland then described a pattern that every returned missionary knows something about. He talked about investigators who feel the enlightenment of the Spirit and who commit to be baptized. Then, they retreat, or pull the plug on their baptismal service and subsequent membership in the Church. Elder Holland said that every missionary knows exactly what he is talking about: "appointments for discussions cancelled, the Book of Mormon in a plastic bag hanging from a front-door knob, [and] baptismal dates not met."[6] Next, Elder Holland transitioned the conversation from missionary work to courtship and engagement:

> I would like to have a dollar for every person in a courtship who knew he or she had felt the guidance of the Lord in that relationship, had prayed about the experience enough to know it was the will of the Lord, knew they loved each other and enjoyed each other's company, and saw a lifetime of wonderful compatibility ahead—only to panic, to get a brain cramp, to have total catatonic fear sweep over them.[7]

---

5. Jeffrey R. Holland, "Cast Not Away Therefore Your Confidence," Brigham Young University Devotional, 2 March 1999; https://speeches.byu.edu/talks/jeffrey-r-holland/cast-not-away-therefore-your-confidence/
6. Ibid.
7. Ibid.

Elder Holland then explained that such couples reconsider the relationship and perhaps postpone the marriage or terminate the relationship completely. After explaining to the Brigham Young University students the need to be both prayerful and careful regarding the marriage decision, Elder Holland then counseled:

> Yes, there are cautions and considerations to make, but once there has been genuine illumination, beware the temptation to retreat from a good thing. If it was right when you prayed about it and trusted it and lived for it, it is right now. Don't give up when the pressure mounts. You can find an apartment. You can win over your mother-in-law. You can sell your harmonica and therein fund one more meal. It's been done before. Don't give in. *Certainly don't give in to that being who is bent on the destruction of your happiness.* He wants everyone to be miserable like unto himself. Face your doubts. Master your fears... Stay the course and see the beauty of life unfold for you.[8]

Like many of you, I have had to rely on Elder Holland's counsel more than once in my life. Making big decisions is a scary responsibility and proposition. Many of us, once we have made a significant decision, often let doubt and uncertainly creep into our minds and hearts. However, Elder Holland's invitation rings true: Do not give into Satan, who wants all of us to be miserable. It is Satan who wants us to doubt, fear, and live in a state of confusion. However, the Lord is full of assurance, peace, love, and light. Therefore, learn to move forward with faith. Have the courage to act on your inspiration and your gut feelings. Do not let Satan win the battle for your happiness. Do not take counsel from your fears.

---

8. Ibid., emphasis in original.

Thought Questions

1. What are some of the doubts and fears you are experiencing regarding the marriage decision?
2. How can the teachings of the gospel of Jesus Christ help you remedy those fears?

19

What if two people receive different answers?

Individuals receiving different answers, different promptings, and different impressions to a similar prayer is not an uncommon phenomenon. For example, as a bishop, I have prayed over the names of individuals for certain callings and felt strongly that a particular sister should serve as Young Women president. Meanwhile, my counselors have also prayed over the same calling and have sometimes come up with different names. Although we all felt inspired in our decision, we recognize that we needed to go back to the "drawing board" to discuss and counsel more and to pray more, until we become unified in our decision. In many cases, the reason we came up with different names is we did not have all of the information that we needed.

This same experience can also occur in the lives of those trying to decide to marry. For example, a man prays over the marriage decision and receives a "yes" answer, while the woman does not receive an answer at all, or in some cases, receives a "no." Of course, there are just as many stories when the woman receives a positive confirmation and the man does not. This may be one of the most difficult concepts to address in this book. In fact, President Dieter F. Utchdorf declared, "Let me tell you that your prayers are heard. Your Father in Heaven knows the desires of your heart. I cannot tell you why one individual's prayers are answered one way while someone else's are answered differently. But this I can tell you: the righteous desires of your hearts will be fulfilled."[1] Some of these issues are so complex that there is not a "one-size-fits-all-answer." Every situation is unique. In fact, if President Utchdorf doesn't know why some prayers are answered differently for each individual, perhaps I should not try to answer this question either. However, since so many of my students have asked me this question over the years, I feel some responsibility to at least share some possibilities—*not answers but possibilities*—in addressing this experience that some LDS couples encounter.

God Tells One "Yes" and Another "No"

I have heard some people speculate that our Father in Heaven may tell one person "yes" and the other person "no" because the potential marriage may be *good* for one person, but *bad* for the other. I understand that our Father in Heaven views us as individuals, but I have to believe He also sees us as couples. It would make little sense to me that a loving Heavenly Father would confuse a couple by providing both of them with contrary revelations.

Why would a loving God tell a woman in a relationship "yes" and her potential fiancé "no?" Although I do not profess to know all of the intricacies of this topic, there is one thing I know for sure—our Father in Heaven is not a God of confusion (1 Corinthians 14:33), and it seems irrational to believe that He would purposely confuse us. In my mind, if the answer is "yes" or "no," then both parties would receive that same answer from a loving God.

---

1. Dieter F. Utchdorf, "Reflection in the Water," *Brigham Young University Speeches*, 1 November 2009.

Other Possibilities

There are a myriad of possibilities of why one person in a relationship could get a different spiritual answer from the inspiration their partner has received. In some cases, one of the individuals in a relationship may *not really* want to receive an answer because 1) they would have to respond to the positive confirmation and 2) ultimately get married. Marriage could be something they may not want to.

Some may worry that if they receive a "no" answer, they would need to terminate the relationship—and they may not want to do that either! In other situations, perhaps the marriage decision is scary for a particular person, and they fear the prospect of marriage. Other individuals are not in spiritual condition to receive an answer from the Lord. Still, others may suppose that they have received an answer from the Spirit, but they actually have not. Perhaps their emotions are driving their decision rather than the Spirit. Let us consider some other possibilities.

1. Lack of understanding on how to receive revelation. In this case, the concept of receiving revelation is new to an individual. That is, they have a small experience base when it comes to obtaining answers from the Lord. These individuals often do not understand how the Spirit works in their lives. Sometimes they are looking for a magnificent, spiritual manifestation. In fact, they may have received revelation but have been unaware that the Spirit was speaking to them. These individuals should spend some time in the scriptures, in this book, other books, conference talks, *Liahona/Ensign* articles, and with spiritual mentors who can help them understand the workings of the Holy Ghost.

2. Unworthiness. Unfortunately, in some cases, couples are not worthy to receive an answer from the Spirit. They have broken the law of chastity or, for other reasons, have separated themselves from their Father in Heaven and the Holy Ghost. As these individuals begin the repentance process, the Spirit will begin to operate in their lives, and their ability to receive clear answers will return to them.

3. Not "studying" out their decision. Perhaps an individual needs more time to really dig in and study out their decision. They need to read the scriptures and their patriarchal blessings. They certainly need to pray with energy and sincerity, as they present their decision to the Lord. These individuals also need to discuss their decision with loving family members, friends, and church leaders whom they respect and trust.

Consider the pros and cons of the decision, as well as the long-term effect that such a choice will have on your life. Take more time to investigate, study, and learn about each other. Continue to date each other, ask each other questions, and spend adequate time together. Perhaps spending more time with them around their family and with their parents can help you see things more clearly. I also recommend that you take the time to study the gospel as a couple, work on projects together, watch someone's children occasionally, serve and help others, take a road trip, and discuss significant topics together. All of these activities will provide the information you need to make the marriage decision much easier.

4. Stewardship in revelation. Although we have discussed this principle already, it is worth repeating. Unless we have responsibility for another person in our family, or ecclesiastically, then we have no right, or ability to receive a revelation for someone else. Just because an individual claims to have received a revelation that you are to marry, you are not bound by that revelation. If the revelation is true, then it will be revealed to both parties.

Is your partner purporting to have received a revelation from God? If they have received a revelation and you have not, or if you have received a different answer, talk to them about their revelation. Learn more about the answer they received, and how they have received it. Their explanation may help you to see things more clearly, one way or the other.

5. *Good old-fashioned fear*. Never make a big decision in your life based on fear. Some people fear they may never have another chance to marry, and so they gamble on a person that may have significant problems. Of course, others stay far away from the marriage decision because of their personal fears.

Fear can also prevent revelation from coming to us. Moreover, fear could cause doubt and confusion over previous revelations or inspiration that has come. Be careful. Fear and doubt can be confused for a "no" answer, when, instead, Satan is simply trying to deceive you. I am not saying that you should not pay attention to doubt and fear, but you certainly should work through it and determine where it is coming from. Sometimes doubt and fear stem from our own anxiety. For example, an individual who experiences anxiety over the marriage decision will likely encounter anxiety in many other aspects of their lives. These individuals are simply "anxious" people. In fact, if they break up with person "A" because of their anxious feelings, they are also likely to experience anxiety with person "B," "C," and "D." I have seen individuals experience this pattern, only to become engaged several times to several people over the course of years and never marry any of them. Looking back, at age thirty-five and still single, these individuals say, "I should have married person 'A' ten years ago."

President James E. Faust explained, "Let us not take counsel from our fears. May we remember always to be of good cheer, put our faith in God, and live worthy for Him to direct us. We are each entitled to receive personal inspiration to guide us through our mortal probation."[2] For those in this situation, identify the sources of the doubt, fear, and anxiety and see if these issues can be addressed or solved. Remember what Michael Wilcox taught—the Lord deals in specifics, not generalities. If your concerns are specific, then pay attention to them and determine if

---

2. James E. Faust, "Be Not Afraid," *Ensign*, October 2002, 6.

those issues can be resolved. If your doubts and fears are more general, then consider that Satan could be trying to deceive you. Push the Deceiver off to the side, and move forward with faith.

On the other hand, if you see some major red flags and other warnings, then pay close attention. Do not jump into a relationship where you have major concerns. From time to time, doubt and fear are legitimate—pay close attention to those feelings. In this case, visit with parents, family members, friends, and leaders. Let them share with you how they feel about the person you are marrying. Listen to them closely. Seek for peace in this decision.

6. *The issue of timing.* It could be likely that the timing of a marriage or the timing of receiving an answer could be right for one person but not the other. Remember the counsel of President Dallin H. Oaks on timing. He said, "In all the important decisions in our lives, what is most important is to *do the right thing.* Second, and only slightly behind the first, is to *do the right thing at the right time.* People who do the right thing at the wrong time can be frustrated and ineffective. They can even be confused about whether they made the right choice when what was wrong was not their choice but their timing."[3]

Perhaps the person you are with is the right person, but maybe the relationship needs more time to develop. Maybe you both need several more months, or even longer, to mature and develop emotionally and spiritually, which will better suit you for married life. Perhaps the timing of the relationship is why you have been finding it difficult to receive an answer. If this is the case, regroup as a couple and redefine the relationship. Set goals in areas where you want to improve and grow, and then go to work. Continue to progress toward marriage. Two of my

---

3. Dallin H. Oaks, "Timing," *Brigham Young University Speeches,* 29 January 2002; https://speeches.byu.edu/talks/dallin-h-oaks/timing/; emphasis in original.

daughters are married to men where, initially, their relationship did not work out. They broke up, and then a year or two later, reconnected, and now are both happily married. For both of them, timing was a major issue!

7. Go toward the light. Sometimes it may seem the Lord is quiet when it comes to our personal marriage decision. In many instances, He may want us to decide. The Lord trusts you, and He may want you to move forward. So, move forward with faith. Trust in the Lord and keep moving toward the marriage alter. Elder Richard G. Scott explained,

> What do you do when you have prepared carefully, have prayed fervently, waited a reasonable time for a response, and still do not feel an answer? You may want to express thanks when that occurs, for it is an evidence of His trust. When you are living worthily and your choice is consistent with the Savior's teachings and you need to act, proceed with trust. As you are sensitive to the promptings of the Spirit, one of two things will certainly occur at the appropriate time: either the stupor of thought will come, indicating an improper choice, or the peace or the burning in the bosom will be felt, confirming that your choice was correct. When you are living righteously and are acting with trust, God will not let you proceed too far without a warning impression if you have made the wrong decision.[4]

If your decision is right, things will work out. If you are on the right path and pressing forward, your relationship and marriage plans will continue to unfold. If your decision is wrong, the Lord will stop you. Keep the commandments and your covenants, move forward with faith, and continue toward your goal of temple marriage. If your decision is wrong, the Lord always has a way of letting you know.

---

4. Richard G. Scott, "Using the Supernal Gift of Prayer," *Ensign*, May 2007.

Elder Boyd K. Packer shared a significant experience many years ago that bears repeating. He had been called to become a General Authority, and his family would need to move from Lindon, Utah, to the Salt Lake City Area. At the time, the Packer's still had a large family, Elder Packer had just finished a doctoral degree, and funds were tight. Finding a home they could afford would be difficult. However, the Packers ultimately did find a home that suited them perfectly. But, in Elder Packer's logical mind, there was no way they could afford the payments. He went to Elder Harold B. Lee for counsel, who suggested that Elder Packer move forward with faith. Since Elder Packer was not quite satisfied with that answer, Elder Lee felt impressed to send him to the prophet, President David O. McKay. The prophet also encouraged Elder Packer to move forward with faith but offered no financial assistance. Elder Packer explained, "I was very willing to be obedient but saw no way possible for me to do as he counseled me to do." Elder Packer then reported to Elder Lee what President McKay had said, stating, "I saw no way to move in the direction I was counseled to go." Elder Harold B. Lee then explained,

> "The trouble with you is you want to see the end from the beginning." I replied that I would like to see at least a step or two ahead. Then came the lesson of a lifetime: "You must learn to walk to the edge of the light, and then a few steps into the darkness; then the light will appear and show the way before you." Then he quoted these 18 words from the Book of Mormon: "Dispute not because ye see not, for ye receive no witness until after the trial of your faith." (Ether 12:6)[5]

---

5. Boyd K. Packer, "The Edge of the Light," *BYU Magazine*, March 1991, magazine.byu.edu; see also Lucile C. Tate, *Boyd K. Packer: Watchman on the Tower* (Salt Lake City: Bookcraft, 1995), 137–38.

WHAT IF TWO PEOPLE RECEIVE DIFFERENT ANSWERS?

Some of us will have to walk to the edge of the light, take several steps into the darkness, and then the light will come. Regarding the marriage decision, sometimes you will have to trust your own intuition and move forward. If you do not understand or cannot comprehend how getting married will even work, exercise faith and move ahead. The Lord will light the way before you, one-step at a time. As the verse says in Ether, sometimes we will receive no answer until we experience a trial of our faith. So, put your best foot forward and get moving. When trials come, sort them out, make sense of them, and see if they can be resolved.

Elder Dieter F. Utchdorf explained, "There are times when we have to step into the darkness in faith, confident that God will place solid ground beneath our feet once we do."[6] If we are on the verge of putting our feet in the wrong place, the Lord will let us know. He will stop us in our tracks. He will not allow us to go astray if we stay close to Him and are obedient to his counsel.

Thought Questions

1. Have you ever been in a relationship where one person received a certain answer from the Spirit, and you received a completely different answer?
2. If you were making the marriage decision and received the answer of "yes," and your potential fiancé received a "no," what would you do to resolve your issues?

---

6. Dieter F. Uchtdorf, "The *Why* of Priesthood Service," *Ensign*, May 2012, 59.

20

Have you ever recorded a personal revelation?

Once you have received revelation, I would admonish you to write down what the Lord has revealed to you. There are many reasons for such a practice. For instance, when difficult times come, or when you begin to feel doubt and fear regarding your marriage decision, reviewing your spiritual experiences could help serve as an anchor and help you remain firm and steadfast in your decision. Remember, almost everyone will experience some kind of doubt, fear, or questions when it comes to the marriage decision. Furthermore, when we record the revelations the Lord gives to us, He will send us more light, information, and knowledge.

Like many of you who are reading this book, I was not baptized in the Church when I was eight years old. Instead, I was eighteen. In fact, I was one month away from beginning my first year of college. I remember my baptism day with fondness and clarity. Looking back, I recognize what was most memorable was not actually my baptism but another event that occurred later that evening. After my baptismal service, many members of our local branch, along with the missionaries, went out to celebrate my joining the Church at a local pizza restaurant. While we were eating, the missionary who baptized me said, "Mark, how do you feel?" I told my missionary friend that I felt wonderful, excited, and probably had never been happier. In fact, I felt the light and love of the gospel of Jesus Christ was oozing out of my pores. Then, the missionary gave me this charge. He said, "When you get home tonight, I want you to write down your feelings about your baptism." I told my missionary friend that I would do exactly what he said. Unfortunately, I never did. For whatever reason, I forgot and forged ahead. Occasionally, I would have thoughts (from the Spirit) that would remind me that I should write down my feelings that transpired on my baptism day, but I never got around to it.

I had wanted to join the Church earlier in my life, but my parents were bitterly opposed to me being baptized. Eventually, after my brief stint in West Texas, I had to return home for a few days before I began attending college in East Texas—as a brand-new member of The Church of Jesus Christ of Latter-day Saints. I did not intend to tell my parents that I was now a member of the Church. In fact, my master plan included informing my parents many years later about my membership. I thought that maybe when my first child was going to be baptized that would be a good time to tell my parents. However, after visiting with my best friend's family who initially introduced me to the gospel, they persuaded me to tell my parents about my conversion immediately.

Therefore, I reluctantly followed their counsel and did tell my parents. Consequently, they were quite upset and wondered if there was anything they could do to "reverse the process" and save me. My mom literally drove me to several ex-Mormons to see if they could convince me to leave the Church. Since I had only been a member for a few weeks, I am sure they supposed I was an easy target. However, I was not rattled and stood my ground as I spoke with these individuals. I feel that having my good friends with me helped immensely. However, I believe I would have fared better if I had followed my missionary's advice and had written down my personal feelings about my baptism. Those feelings would have been nice to review during this process.

Several months later, a stronger wave hit me that practically knocked me over. I was sitting in my dorm room on my college campus. It was a Saturday afternoon, and I was doing some homework, along with my faithful LDS roommate. Someone knocked on our dorm room door, so I answered it. Surprisingly, it was my uncle and his son (my cousin.) They had driven several hours to come and visit me. Each of them held a stack of books in their arms and looked ready for a "showdown." My uncle was an associate pastor at his evangelical church and had been "prepping for months" to come and save me from the "Mormons." I am sure he had come at my parents' urging. Undoubtedly, they felt they had to intervene before I left on my mission. Had my roommate, who was a seasoned member of the Church, not been there that day, I may not have spiritually survived. I could not answer most of my uncle's difficult questions and accusations, but my roommate could, and he did. Nevertheless, my uncle sowed a substantial amount of doubt in my young LDS mind, which became filled with confusion and darkness. It took me about two weeks to recover from the message he delivered. Once again, had I recorded the feelings I had at my baptism, I could have brushed my uncle's conversation off to the side and would not have been shaken by his anti-Mormon propaganda. Thankfully, after a week or two of immersing myself back into the scriptures and discussing issues with my roommate, I was able to land back on my spiritual feet.

Nevertheless, I learned a great lesson. We should always record our spiritual feelings in some kind of journal or book of remembrance. We may need to rely on those words, much like we would rely on or receive strength from our patriarchal blessing promises, or the scriptures. This was a hard lesson for me, but I grew from the experience. Over the years, I have grown and recognized the wisdom in writing down our spiritual impressions. I have recorded most of the significant experiences that have occurred with my family.

On one occasion, Joseph Smith taught the Twelve Apostles,

> If you assemble from time to time, and proceed to discuss important questions, and pass decisions upon the same, and fail to note them down, by and by you will be driven to straits from which you will not be able to extricate yourselves, because you may be in a situation not to bring your faith to bear with sufficient perfection or power to obtain the desired information; or, perhaps, for neglecting to write these things when God had revealed them, not esteeming them of sufficient worth, the Spirit may withdraw and God may be angry; and there is, or was, a vast knowledge, of infinite importance, which is now lost.[1]

This statement from the Prophet describes my situation perfectly. I failed to "note down" important experiences during my conversion process and consequently was almost not able to "extricate" myself from the mess I had encountered.

Similarly, Elder Neal A. Maxwell explained, "We should learn, too, that the prompting that goes unresponded to may not be repeated. Writing down what we have been prompted with is vital. A special thought can also be lost later in the day in the rough and tumble of life. God should not, and may not, chose to repeat the prompting if we assign what was given such a low priority as to put it aside."[2] Life is busy, and quite often we forget the spiritual experiences that have transpired in our lives. If you are engaged in the marriage decision, I strongly recommend that you record the positive promptings that come to your mind and

---

1. Joseph Smith, from minutes of Instruction to the Council of the Twelve, 27 February 1835; *History of the Church,* 2:198–99.
2. Neal A. Maxwell, *Wherefore Ye Must Press Forward,* 122.

heart. Those sacred words and thoughts could be a tremendous blessing to you several months down the road.

Recording Inspiration

Over the years, I heard Elder Richard G. Scott teach about the importance of recording our spiritual impressions. At a Brigham Young University Education Week, Elder Scott taught:

> I notice that many of you have come prepared to take notes on what you hear. While that is of great benefit, I will share a pattern that will provide you even greater access to truth. It is summarized in this statement of principle: *Throughout the remainder of my life, I will seek to learn by what I hear, see, and feel. I will write down the important things I learn, and I will do them.*[3]

Doing the things that the Lord reveals to us will also build a sacred trust between Him and us. Ultimately, the Lord will know that He can trust us with any message He shares with us.

Elder Scott additionally taught that as we record impressions from the Holy Ghost, more inspiration will come to us that we would not have otherwise received. Hence, by recording the revelations we receive, the Lord will trust us enough to share more light and knowledge with us. On another occasion, Elder Scott taught, "Record impressions of the Spirit. Inspiration carefully recorded shows God that His communications are sacred to us. Recording will also enhance our ability to recall revelation."[4] He also stated, "Knowledge carefully recorded is knowledge available in time of need."[5]

---

3. Richard G. Scott, "To Learn and to Teach More Effectively," *Brigham Young University Speeches*, 21 August 2007, BYU Education Week, 2.
4. Richard G. Scott, "How to Obtain Revelation and Inspiration for Your Personal Life," *Ensign*, May 2012, 46.
5. Richard G. Scott, *Ensign*, November 1993, 86–88.

Elder Scott provided another advantage to recording revelation. He stated that if we record the messages we receive, then the following will happen:

> The spiritual knowledge you gain will be available throughout your life. Always, day or night, wherever you are, whatever you are doing, seek to recognize and respond to the direction of the Spirit. Have available a piece of paper or a card to record such guidance. Express gratitude to the Lord for the spiritual guidance you receive and obey it. This practice will reinforce your capacity to learn by the Spirit. It will enhance the guidance of the Lord in your life. You will learn more as you act upon the knowledge, experience, and inspiration communicated to you by the Holy Ghost.[6]

Over the years, I have come to learn that many of the strongest Saints I know keep a record or journal of the inspiration that comes to them. I have learned of individuals who keep a notebook near their nightstand, or close to the shower, so that when they received ideas and impressions, they could remember them and act on them. As a bishop, I often felt overwhelmed with the revelation that came regularly. I also learned that I could not remember things as well as I once did. I began the practice of recording these thoughts or flashes of inspiration in a small notebook that I carried with me at all times. Often, even as I exercised, I would receive impressions from the Holy Ghost. I would stop what I was doing and write down the inspiration. In due time, I was able to act on these promptings from the Spirit, which certainly benefitted our ward, and in many cases, our family.

Second, make it a practice to continue to write down the spiritual impressions for the remainder of your life. Those thoughts

---

6. Scott, "To Learn and to Teach More Effectively," *Brigham Young University Speeches*, 21 August 2007, BYU Education Week, 2.

and impressions will become your own veritable Liahona, which will provide safety, guidance, and direction throughout your life. As you record these impressions, the Lord will continue to flood your mind and heart with more direction that will bless you, your family, and those you serve.

Thought Questions

1. When was the last time you felt the Lord speaking to you, providing guidance to you, or giving you direction? What was the message?
2. Will you consider writing down the revelations you receive? I invite you to do that today. As you do so, more revelation will come to you.

Conclusion: Are you ready to move forward with faith?

The journey to marriage can be one of the most exciting adventures life has to offer. Sometimes you will experience the highest of highs, and occasionally, the lowest of lows. Nevertheless, our Father in Heaven will be with you in this journey. I assure you that He wants you to be married in the holy temple to a righteous companion, and He wants you to raise a righteous family. He will walk alongside you in this process. He will not leave you alone!

I know that if we are humble, our Father in Heaven will lead us by the hand and give us answers to our prayers (see D&C 112:10). Sometimes "humble" could be translated as "open-minded." When it comes to finding a marriage partner, we should be willing to go where the Lord will take us. With open minds, the Lord could lead us to people, places, and time lines that we never imagined.

I close this book with a statement from one of my favorite people—George Q. Cannon. As a member of the First Presidency, he taught:

> No matter how serious the trial, how deep the distress, how great the affliction, [God] will never desert us. He never has, and He never will. He cannot do it. It is not His character [to do so]. He is an unchangeable being; the same yesterday, the same today, and He will be the same throughout the eternal ages to come. We have found that God. We have made Him our friend, by obeying His Gospel; and He will stand by us.

We may pass through the fiery furnace; we may pass through deep waters; but we shall not be consumed nor overwhelmed. We shall emerge from all these trials and difficulties the better and purer for them, if we only trust in our God and keep His commandments.[1]

Our Heavenly Father will always be available to us. He wants to help you in this journey toward eternal marriage. He will provide you with guidance, strength, and direction. He will walk with you on this journey, and He will never abandon you. He will bless you in ways you have never imagined if you will trust in Him, believe in Him, and always desire to follow Him. His richest and deepest blessings are for those who will always honor Him.

---

1. George Q. Cannon, "Freedom of the Saints," in Collected Discourses, comp. Brian H. Stuy, 5 vols. (1987–92), 2:185; emphasis added.

About the Author

Mark D. Ogletree joined the Church at age eighteen. He served an LDS mission from 1982–1984 in Seattle, Washington. He earned a bachelor of arts degree in 1987 from Brigham Young University; master of arts in educational psychology from Northern Arizona University in 1990; master of arts in mental health counseling in 1994 from Northern Arizona University; and a PhD in family and human development from Utah State University in May 2000.

Mark has taught at Brigham Young University in the Church History and Doctrine Department since 2010. He has published several books and articles on marriage and family relationships.